The Carry-On Traveller

The Ultimate Guide to Packing Light

By Erin McNeaney

Cover design by Emir Orucevic.

Visit the author's website at www.NeverEndingVoyage.com.

ISBN: 153691374X
ISBN-13: 978-1536913743

To Simon, who makes everything possible.

CONTENTS

INTRODUCTION

We all love the excitement, adventure, and relaxation of travel; many of us even relish the anticipation of the planning stages. But I've never met anyone who enjoys packing, an essential but often stressful part of any trip. There's the indecision over what to bring, the struggle to cram everything into your luggage, and the hassle of lugging your heavy bags around—in and out of cars, on and off buses, up and down stairs. It's a burden when you want to get on with having fun.

Thankfully, it doesn't have to be like this.

Packing light is the secret to stress-free travel, and travelling with just a carry-on-size bag—one you can take on planes—is best of all. Travelling with such a small bag may seem restrictive, but it actually gives you more freedom, liberating you from the burden of stuff. You'll save time at airports, avoid wasting money on checked luggage fees (which are increasingly common), and reduce the stress of hauling bulky suitcases. Packing and carrying your bag will no longer be something you dread. You can focus on experiencing new places instead.

This book is for everyone who has struggled with packing and wished they could travel with a lighter load. You'll learn how travelling with just a carry-on is possible for every traveller, experienced or newbie, young or old, whether you are planning a weekend in Paris or a year-long trip around the world.

Why I Love Carry-On Travel

I know it's possible because I've been travelling the world nonstop for six years with a carry-on backpack. My partner Simon and I left the UK in 2010 after selling everything we owned to become digital nomads. We run a business online creating iPhone apps and writing about our experiences on our popular travel blog, Never Ending Voyage.

Simon and I didn't start our travelling lives with a carry-on. Our first backpacking trip was a month-long train journey around Europe when we were 19 years old. We made all the usual mistakes—packing far too much and taking things like sleep sheets we never used. We learned what we did and didn't need, and on each subsequent trip our backpacks became lighter as we grew more confident living with less.

In 2007, we left on our big adventure—a year travelling around the world. Our luggage wasn't carry-on only, but our 65-litre backpacks contained far less stuff than we'd left behind in our three-bedroom house in Manchester.

When we returned to the UK, I was shocked and horrified by how much we owned—why on earth did I need four hairbrushes and 30 t-shirts? After living out of a backpack, it was overwhelming. We filled bags with clothes for the charity shop. We just didn't need them anymore.

That realisation was the starting point for our minimalism journey, which led to us selling our belongings and heading off with a backpack again 15 months later. This time our bags were even smaller, and armed with a one-way ticket to Rio de Janeiro, we had no plans to return.

We've now been travelling for six years. All our possessions fit in a single carry-on backpack each, and we haven't missed owning more. I wrote this book because after years of travelling with hand luggage, I am convinced it's the best way to travel. I am happy with the decision every time I whiz through an airport in ten minutes while others are crowding around the baggage carousel, every time I waltz onto a bus without worrying if my bag will emerge from the luggage storage at the end of the journey, and every time I walk anywhere for more than a few minutes with my backpack.

I've been grateful for my small bag when clambering in and out of tiny boats while island hopping in Thailand, when learning to sail a yacht in Malaysia and staying in a cupboard-size cabin, and when walking to a bus station in Mexico as all the taxis were full. I've been in so many situations that would have been a huge hassle with a lot of luggage but were no problem with one small backpack.

Travelling light was the best decision I made when I started travelling. I've saved myself money, time, stress, and backache. Most importantly, I've gained freedom—I can pack all my belongings in ten minutes and head off on the next adventure.

I want to share what I've learnt to help you lessen your load so you can focus on the joy of travel.

What You'll Learn in *The Carry-On Traveller*

This book covers everything you need to know to pack lighter. In Part 1 you'll learn the many benefits of carry-on only travel, the basic principles you can apply to any trip, and the airline restrictions you need to know before you fly (including my tips on how to get away with a bag that's over the weight limit). You'll find out how to choose the luggage that's right for you, including the pros and cons of backpacks versus suitcases, and one bag versus two. There are detailed reviews of my favourite backpacks and recommendations from other travellers for ideal carry-on suitcases.

In Part 2 we get down to the nitty-gritty—what to pack. You'll discover the best travel fabrics, the brands that make practical yet stylish travel clothes, and how to select a colour scheme so you can mix and match all your clothes. You'll see that travelling with less doesn't mean you have to give up your individual style—fashionable carry-on travel is certainly possible. The detailed clothes packing lists for women and men can be adapted to suit your personal tastes and trip type, including cold-weather travel.

Most people travel with at least one electronic device these days, and the detailed electronics section will help you decide what you really need. I discuss the pros and cons of travelling with a laptop, smartphone, tablet, e-reader, and various types of cameras (including recommended models). You'll learn how to back up your data, the best way to use a mobile phone abroad, and the most useful apps.

I suggest what to pack in your toiletry and medical kit, how to manage airline liquid restrictions so you don't have to go without your favourite beauty products, and the best small but useful miscellaneous items like duct tape. You'll find out how to access your cash on the road, the best bank accounts to avoid international fees, and the safest way to store your money and passport.

You'll also learn what *not* to pack—the items that often appear on packing lists but the vast majority of travellers don't need. That said, just because you are travelling carry-on only doesn't mean you can't fit in some luxury items— things you don't *really* need but are important to you—and there are suggestions for travel with a musical instrument and yoga mat.

In Part 3 you'll see why *how* you pack is just as important as *what* you pack. I review packing cubes and organisers and explain how they help you fit more in your carry-on. You'll learn how to pack efficiently and why a packing list and test pack are important parts of the process. I address common concerns like how to do laundry on the road, keeping your gear safe, and the best travel insurance.

For Part 4, I interviewed a range of carry-on travellers—fashion and makeup lovers, families, solo travellers, couples, campers, photographers, and even an artist in his 70s—who share their tips on packing light to show it's possible for everyone, whatever your circumstances.

Finally, in the Appendix, you'll find our complete packing list, useful packing resources, packing lists from a variety of carry-on travellers, and the carry-on size and weight restrictions for many airlines.

Packing light will revolutionise your travel experience. I hope you enjoy the book and feel inspired to try carry-on travel on your next trip.

Recommended Resources

I have created a resource page at carryontravels.com listing all the gear and resources I recommend in the book, divided by chapter. You will also find photos of our gear, our most up-to-date packing list, discounts for our favourite items, and a downloadable packing list to use for your next trip.

PART ONE
Getting Started

1. Why Travel with Only Carry-On Luggage?

Travelling with a small carry-on bag may seem challenging, but the benefits make it worthwhile.

Less Stress

Life with less is simpler. One bag is easier to keep track of on hectic travel days than multiple bulky suitcases. You can move faster and navigate new cities without standing out as much. You can walk around searching for the best accommodation, squeeze on a crowded bus, and run to catch a train—tasks that would be stressful, or impossible, with a large amount of luggage.

Save Money

Travelling with hand luggage only saves you money. Many airlines charge for checking in luggage; you avoid these costs travelling with a carry-on. Checking in each bag for each leg of your trip can cost $25 or more, so the savings add up.

When you have less to carry you are more likely to walk or take public transport to your accommodation rather than taking expensive taxis, saving even more cash.

Travelling light stops you from buying things you don't need. When space is limited you are much more conscious about your purchases. You'll learn to only shop to swap—to replace items in your bag when needed, not add to them.

More Security

When you only have one bag to worry about, it's easier to keep it safe. My backpack is never out of my sight on transport, whereas large luggage is usually stored away from passengers.

Whenever you check in luggage, especially when you have flight connections, there's a risk the airline could lose your bag—SITA reported that in 2014, 24.1 million bags were lost, delayed, or damaged by airlines around the world. When you take it on the plane, you know it'll be there when you arrive.

You can also keep a carry-on bag with you on buses. It's more secure to keep it under your seat than thrown on top or underneath a bus, where anyone getting off at earlier stops can access it.

Save Time

At Airports - I appreciate my carry-on bag the most when I stumble bleary-eyed off a long flight and stroll straight out of the airport, past the crowds gathering at the luggage carousels. This is a huge bonus after an exhausting journey when all you want to do is get to your hotel as soon as possible.

A carry-on also saves time checking in at airports. Most airlines offer online check-in, so when you arrive at the airport, you can skip the long lines and go straight to security.

At Bus Stations - This works for buses too, and it is especially useful when touts gather around arriving buses to bombard you with offers of taxis and hotels as you collect your luggage. With your bag in hand, you can make a quick escape before the touts even notice you.

Packing - Packing is a chore most people dread. I'm not a huge fan either, but when you have less stuff and a good system for organising it in your luggage, packing becomes a 10-minute task.

Finding Things - When you own less, you can find things more quickly. The more stuff we have, the harder it is to find, which wastes time and adds stress to our lives. Who wants that when we're exploring the world?

Dressing - A lack of clothes is one of the biggest concerns of people considering travelling with a carry-on, but there is a surprising advantage to having less choice—less time spent deciding what to wear. When you only have a few outfits, it is obvious what to wear in every situation. I don't miss having dozens of outfits—lots of clothes are a burden more than a blessing.

Reduce Back Pain

If you're travelling with a backpack, your back will thank you for travelling light; you'll no longer have a heavy load weighing you down and leaving you with an aching back and shoulders. Suitcase users benefit too. A smaller, lighter suitcase is easier to roll around, carry up stairs, and lift in and out of transport, and it will put less pressure on your arms and back.

It's Liberating

Liberating is the word I've heard new carry-on travellers use the most to describe their lightened load. It's a revelation to discover how little we need. When you eliminate things that don't add value to your life, it's enormously liberating. You aren't tied down by your possessions. You can leave anywhere quickly and go wherever you want. The freedom is intoxicating.

"But I'll Have Less Stuff!"

The downside of travelling with a carry-on bag is having less choice of things, but I've found the benefits far outweigh this disadvantage. Most people adapt and find having less stuff a positive rather than a negative. I can't imagine travelling, or living, any other way.

2. Basic Principles of Travelling with a Carry-On

These basic principles make travelling with hand luggage possible and can be applied to any trip. I'll go into detail about the concepts later, but for now, they'll start you thinking about ways you could pack lighter.

You Don't Need as Much as You Think

The first step to packing light is to change your mindset and realise you don't need as much as you think. This is difficult at first, but it's a gradual process—with time it becomes easier and you'll adapt to having less. As you start reducing the amount you pack, you'll discover what you *really* need and how easy and liberating it is to live with less.

Thousands of other travellers manage with a carry-on, so why can't you? What's the worst that can happen if you have less stuff than you're used to? Give carry-on travel a try, and you'll soon wonder what on earth you packed in those heavy suitcases.

Pack the Same for a Week or a Year

It makes no difference whether you are packing for a week, month, or year.

I've been travelling for six years with no more than I would pack for a week in Europe.

Pack for a week, and on longer trips do laundry. In many parts of the world there are inexpensive laundry services, or you can hand-wash clothes in your hotel sink. You don't need to launder items as often as you might at home. As long as you shower regularly, washing after one wear is a waste (unless you've been doing some serious sweating). In Part 3 I explain how to keep your clothes fresh and do laundry on the road.

Don't Take Anything "Just in Case"

The best way to reduce your luggage is to avoid packing things "just in case." Everything needs to earn its place in your bag by being used regularly. Don't take hiking boots because you *might* go on a hike when you are spending most of your time in cities. You don't need a jacket if the first three months of your trip are in sunny Southeast Asia. Snorkelling gear? Rent it there. Those high heels in case you're invited to a fancy party? Pack more versatile flats or sandals instead.

Be careful in outdoor shops. It's easy to be sucked in by the array of gear and feel an urgent need for that huge first aid kit, sleeping bag, or mosquito net. You don't need them.

Buy It There

If you do discover you left something behind, most things are available around the world. Other nationalities need warm clothes, umbrellas, toothpaste, and shampoo too. Realising this stops you from panic-packing items you "might" need. If you miss it, buy it locally.

Limit Shoes

Shoes are heavy—don't take more than two or three pairs (including the ones on your feet). Simon has smart hiking shoes and sports sandals. I started with the same but added ballet flats for dressier occasions. Three pairs of shoes may seem restrictive, but with the right choices, that's all you need for most situations. The best shoes for you depend on the type of trip and climate—I discuss the options later in the book.

Mix and Match Your Clothes

Travelling with a carry-on means you'll have fewer clothes than you're used to —around ten items is usually sufficient. Maybe this worries you, but you will adapt and even embrace your simpler collection.

The key to making the most of a limited wardrobe is to ensure all your clothes go together. You should be able to wear every top with every bottom. Keep it simple and pick a colour scheme for your main items. Your outer layers and shoes need to work with everything, so a neutral colour is best.

By mixing and matching, you maximise your choices—four tops and four bottoms make 16 possible outfits. Add lightweight accessories like jewellery and scarves to further change your look.

Look for Small Alternatives

Small alternatives make carry-on travel easier. Due to airline restrictions, you'll need to take small bottles of toiletries (maximum 100 ml/3.4 oz). Travel and outdoor gear is often lighter and less bulky than regular clothes. In South America, my water-resistant windbreaker compressed to the size of an apple and weighed almost nothing. On a Finland ski trip, my ultralight down jacket kept me warm but packed down small. A microfibre travel towel is smaller, lighter, and dries more quickly than a regular towel. A collapsible water bottle will take up less space when empty than a solid one. Whatever you want to pack, you can usually find a lighter, more compact version.

Go Paperless

Going paperless reduces your luggage weight significantly. If you love to read, a Kindle or other e-reader is perfect. You can fit thousands of books on a small device that's lighter than one paperback. Instead of heavy paper guidebooks, buy digital versions for your smartphone, tablet, or e-reader. Artists can try drawing with a multifunctional tablet and stylus rather than a sketchpad. Store your itinerary on your phone and take photos of documents instead of printing them. Paper is heavy—do what you can to minimise the amount you pack.

Pack Multipurpose Items

Choose items with multiple uses. A smartphone is an alarm, calculator, camera, book, and much more. A sarong can be a skirt, beach coverup, towel, or sheet. Shampoo bars can be used as shampoo, soap, and laundry detergent. A reversible skirt or bikini will give you two outfits for the space of one. Duct tape will fix almost anything, as well as work as a bandage, blister tape, sink plug, and lint remover.

Wear Your Heaviest Clothes on Travel Days

On travel days, wear your heaviest items, such as hiking shoes, jeans, and sweaters, to save space and weight in your carry-on. This is especially important when flying on airlines with a low carry-on weight allowance and when travelling to cold climates with bulky winter clothes.

This strategy is trickier in hot countries if you are travelling on transport without air conditioning or walking in the heat to find accommodation. In this case, make sure all your clothes fit in your bag even when you're wearing a lightweight outfit.

Share with Your Partner

Travelling as a couple is easier because you can share items like toiletries and electronics. That's not to say carry-on travel can't be done as a solo traveller (many people do), but if you are travelling with a partner, utilise this advantage and don't double up on items.

Packing for Short Trips Versus Long-Term Travel

The advice in this book is aimed at long-term travellers on trips of over a month because that's what I know. All the tips I share apply to short trips— whether it's a weekend in New York or two weeks in Tuscany—and the good news is that packing carry-on only is even easier, and you can break some of the rules.

On short trips, you know where you'll be travelling, what the weather will be like, and what activities you'll be doing. You can target your packing list to your destination—there's no point packing jeans for the Thai islands, or a bikini and sarong for Rome. If you are visiting a city and know you won't be hiking, you can replace the sports shoes with a pretty pair of flats or sandals. For cooler climates, you can wear your jacket and even a pair of high-heel boots on the plane and not worry about packing them.

You don't need to follow the advice in this book as strictly on short trips. On a week-long holiday you won't need to do laundry, so it doesn't matter if your clothes are quick drying.

You are less likely to be working, so you can reduce your electronics and only pack a smartphone and e-reader, or take a digital detox and leave it all behind (although I wouldn't survive without my Kindle!).

You'll be aware of the conditions at your destination. For a short trip to a European city, I wouldn't worry about power cuts, so I'd leave my head torch (flashlight) behind. I would also be unlikely to need my cable lock (unless staying in hostels), duct tape, sarong, and sewing kit.

For trips of less than a week, you'll be able to pack even fewer clothes than I've listed in this book. For trips of two to four days, Simon and I manage with one backpack between us and have plenty of room to spare. We leave our laptops behind, wear our one pair of shoes, and pack a change or two of clothes, basic toiletries, and our Kindle and iPad. Sometimes I leave my camera behind and use our iPhone. We feel free when we travel like this— getting around is easy, and we can spend a day sightseeing before checking into a hotel without our luggage being a burden.

By targeting your packing list to your destination, you reduce unnecessary gear and can either travel ultralight or add luxury items like dressier clothes for going out.

However long you plan to be away, carry-on only travel will make your experience more enjoyable.

3. Understanding Airline Restrictions

Before you choose your carry-on luggage, you need to be familiar with airline restrictions, as only bags of a certain size and weight can be taken on planes.

Size

The most commonly allowed size of carry-on luggage (also called "cabin baggage" or "hand luggage") is 56 x 36 x 23 cm (22 x 14 x 9 inches) including all handles, side pockets, and wheels. This varies by airline, with some allowing slightly larger or smaller bags, so check with the ones you plan to travel on. In Appendix C, I list the allowances for many airlines.

Airlines have luggage sizers at the gate; when you are boarding the plane they could ask you to place your bag inside. If it doesn't fit, you could be forced to check the bag in the luggage hold (and some airlines charge fees for this). I've found that most airlines aren't too strict about the exact size of your carry-on. In six years, we've never had our bags measured, although Simon's backpack is a few centimetres larger than some airlines allow.

To be sure, it's best to choose luggage within the limits of the airlines you'll be travelling on. If you'll be travelling with a backpack, look for one in the range of 30 to 45 litres, but do check the dimensions as well, and be aware of how overpacking can expand the backpack over the stated measurements.

It's a good idea to board the plane as early as possible because the overhead bins can fill up, and some airlines (like Ryanair and EasyJet) don't guarantee space for your carry-on, even if you meet the restrictions. I've never been unable to find a place for my bag, but if you are worried you can pay extra for priority boarding, which many budget airlines offer.

Weight

Carry-on luggage usually has a weight restriction from 5 kg (11 lb) to 12 kg (26 lb), with most airlines in Asia and Australia limiting it to 7 kg (15 lb). This is a challenge for many people, as by the time you add up the weight of your bag, and maybe a laptop and camera, it doesn't leave much of your allowance for other things.

My bag weighs around 8 kg (18 lb) and Simon's is 10 kg (22 lb), so we are over the limits for many airlines we fly on. But in six years our carry-ons have never been weighed. We aim to be inconspicuous—if the bag doesn't look big and heavy, the airline is less likely to weigh it. It helps that we carry a backpack, as suitcases are heavier and more noticeable.

These tips will help you reduce the weight of your luggage and avoid having it weighed at the airport:

Check in online - The check-in desk is where your bag is in most danger of being weighed. To avoid it, check in online and print your boarding pass (we use internet cafes or ask at our hotel), or save it on your phone if the airline allows it. When you arrive at the airport, you can head straight for security.

One bag - If you travel with just one bag you'll be less conspicuous. The airline will focus on people who look loaded down with luggage.

Use your personal item - Some airlines allow an extra personal item (see below for details). In this case, if you have to use the check-in desk and are travelling with one bag, remove something heavy from your luggage, like a laptop, camera, or packing cube. You can return it to your bag after you've checked in. You can also do this if your baggage is weighed at the gate—there's no need to check your luggage if you haven't maximised your personal item allowance. If you already have a second bag, put your heaviest items in it. Most airlines don't include your personal item in the weight limit, but check before you fly, as a few do.

Wear it - Wear your heaviest clothes and shoes on the plane. If it's too warm to wear your sweater or jacket, carry it or tie it around your waist rather than pack it.

Compress - Pack your bag carefully so it looks less bulky. Use packing cubes or compression bags to reduce the size of your clothes (see 14 - How to Pack) and compress the straps on the outside of your backpack to make it smaller. If it doesn't look big, the airline might not suspect it's overweight.

Fill your pockets - If the airline is very strict, you could fill your pockets with your heavier items—cargo pants or a jacket with pockets would be ideal. I've never had to do this, but Benny Lewis managed to carry on 15 kg (33 lb) of gear in his jacket!

Try a different agent - If your luggage is weighed and you are told to check it in, tell the check-in agent that you need to go and reorganise your gear. When you return to the queue, try to see a different agent, as they might not weigh your bag—it's really the luck of the draw. A friend has done this successfully.

The worst case scenario is your bag is weighed and you're forced to check it in. Have a backup plan for this situation. Ours is to rearrange our valuables in one of our backpacks to carry on and check the other, or if necessary, carry our laptops on the plane and check both bags. Luckily, we've never had to do so.

Don't let the weight issue stop you travelling with a carry-on. Try to keep the weight down (the advice in this book will help) and apply the above tips. Remember that if you do have to check it in, it's unlikely to happen on every flight, and it's better than having to check your luggage all the time.

Personal Item

Most airlines allow one piece of carry-on luggage plus an additional personal item which must fit under the seat in front of you. Some airlines permit any small bag, including a backpack, handbag, laptop case, or shoulder bag; others only allow a small purse or handbag. Check with the airline you'll be travelling with for the size and weight limit for personal items.

As not all airlines allow personal items, especially low-cost airlines, I think it's best to manage without a second bag. See my thoughts on one bag or two in the next chapter.

In addition to your carry-on and personal item, you are sometimes allowed extra articles such as a jacket, umbrella, small bag of food, and bag of duty-free items. If weight is a concern, carry rather than pack these things to maximise your allowance.

Restricted Items

For security reasons, airlines restrict the items you are allowed to carry on the plane; therefore, you need to be more careful than if you were checking in your luggage.

Liquid Restrictions

- All liquids must be in containers with a maximum size of 100 ml (3.4 oz) each.
- Liquids include gels, creams, pastes, and aerosols—shampoo, toothpaste, mascara, perfume, contact lens solution, and liquid foods like jams and sauces are all restricted.
- All liquids must fit in a single, transparent, resealable plastic bag with a maximum volume of one litre (one quart) and a maximum size of 20 x 20 cm. The US doesn't give the required bag size, but a one-quart zip-lock bag is typically 7 x 7.75 inches. You need to be able to close the bag, so don't overstuff it.
- Only one plastic bag of liquids per passenger is allowed.
- You usually have to take the liquid bag out of your luggage when going through security, but not all countries enforce this.

Liquid medications (with a supporting prescription or doctor's note), baby milk, formula, and food are allowed in larger-size bottles and don't need to fit inside the plastic bag, but they must be declared for inspection at airport security.

Don't panic about these liquid rules—in the Toiletries chapter you'll learn how to manage the limit. Most of the time, we travel with one small zip-lock bag of liquids between us, and it's never a problem.

Bonus tip: Water in airports is overpriced. I save money and reduce plastic waste by finishing my water before security and packing the empty plastic bottle. I can then refill it at water fountains or bathrooms on the other side. Of course, this only works in countries where tap water is drinkable.

Other Restricted Items

Weapons, sharp objects, and many sports items such as hiking poles, rackets, and bats are restricted. This includes straight razor blades, scissors, and knives. You can travel with small round-ended or blunt scissors and knives with blades less than 6 cm (2.4 inches) long.

Lighters and non-safety matches are not allowed, but safety matches are.

Although you can take a camping stove in your carry-on, it must be empty of all fuel and cleaned until there are no vapours or residue left. You cannot simply empty the fuel container; this will leave flammable vapours behind. Fuel containers are not allowed.

You can take disposable razors (the type where you replace either just the cartridge or the whole thing), nail clippers and files, tweezers, plastic knives, and sewing needles. We've never had a problem taking these on planes, even in the US, which has the strictest regulations.

If you're not sure if you can take something on the plane, look on the Transportation Security Administration (TSA) website or download the My TSA app. Although this applies to the US, they have the strictest rules; if they allow it, most places will.

The item most travellers are concerned about is a penknife, which appears on many packing lists. I used to travel with a penknife but haven't missed it since I left it behind to travel with a carry-on. I often rent apartments or stay in hostels with kitchens where knives are provided. I travel with a plastic knife (a free one from a takeaway) for the rare occasion I need a knife for a picnic lunch. It works fine for cutting bread, cheese, and tomatoes.

Jenny from Till the Money Runs Out says:

"I am a HUGE fan of pocket knives, and so is Tom. We both always had a pocket knife before we started travelling and at the beginning checked one of our bags so that we could continue carrying a knife. It became just 'not worth it' pretty quickly, and we ditched the knife in favour of carry-on only bags.

"When we were in South America and travelling overland, we did buy a mediocre pocket knife for about $10. We decided that if we ever really wanted a knife, we would buy one and then give it to someone else before boarding our next flight. It still ends up cheaper and easier than checking a bag just for the knife. Though I prefer having one, it's amazing how quickly we got used to making do without."

4. Choosing Your Carry-On Luggage

One Bag or Two?

You might be wondering what to do about a day bag when travelling with a carry-on. As some airlines allow a personal item, it is possible to travel with two bags—your main piece of carry-on luggage and a smaller backpack or bag—but I prefer to travel with just one bag.

Travelling with one bag means less luggage to worry about, it's easier to carry around, and it gives you the flexibility to travel on airlines that only allow one piece of baggage. It avoids the "double turtle" look that many backpackers sport—one backpack on their back and another on their front—which is hot, uncomfortable, and, quite frankly, looks ridiculous.

Travelling with one bag doesn't mean you won't have a smaller bag for sightseeing. The solution is a packable day bag that fits inside your main bag on travel days. This could be a tote bag, cotton shoulder bag, or packable daypack. Packable daypacks are ultralight backpacks that compress into a tiny pouch. The lightest models don't have much support but are fine for carrying a few items. Packable backpacks to look out for include the Sea to Summit Ultra-Sil Day Pack (extremely lightweight), Eagle Creek Packable Daypack, REI Flash 18 Pack, ChicoBag Travel Pack, and the Tortuga Packable Daypack (a good option if you want more features and comfort).

Simon and I share one day bag—a lightweight, cotton shoulder bag that we either pack inside Simon's backpack or use on long bus journeys to store snacks and water. It has a zippered opening and a long strap so I can wear it across my body for extra security, and unlike a backpack, it's easy to carry along with my main backpack when needed. These kinds of bags are available inexpensively in many countries. I like taking advantage of beautiful local textiles—I've bought them in India, Thailand, Guatemala, and Indonesia so far. When we need a more robust bag for a long hike or to take our laptops to work in a cafe, I empty my backpack (simple with the packing cube system I'll discuss later) and use that.

It is possible to travel with two bags—such as a daypack and rolling suitcase or laptop bag and backpack—and you'll see in the Interviews section and packing lists in Appendix B that many carry-on travellers do. Simon even travelled with a backpack plus a travel guitar for our first year on the road. But be aware that you might have issues with certain airlines. I recommend travelling with one bag for the most freedom and flexibility.

Which Type of Luggage? Backpack Versus Rolling Suitcase

Your carry-on luggage options include a backpack, rolling suitcase, or duffel bag. Most round-the-world travellers choose a backpack, while those on shorter trips or with back issues often prefer a suitcase. A non-wheeled duffel bag isn't recommended unless your bag is very light and you'll carry it infrequently.

The luggage you choose depends on personal preference, where you are going, and what activities you'll be doing. If you are flying between cities and taking taxis to your hotel, a suitcase will be fine. If you'll be walking around with your luggage, especially on uneven ground, a backpack is a better option.

Backpack Pros

- Lighter than a suitcase
- More convenient for climbing stairs
- No problems on cobbled and unpaved roads
- Both hands are free
- Easier to move quickly and navigate through a crowd
- You can empty it and use it as a daypack

Backpack Cons

- Weight on your back can be uncomfortable
- Not suitable for people with back problems
- More of a hassle to carry around airports

Rolling Suitcase Pros

- No weight on your back
- Easier in long airport lines
- Doubles as a chair!

Rolling Suitcase Cons

- Heavier than a backpack, so it uses more of your weight allowance
- Difficult to carry up stairs
- Difficult to roll on cobbled streets and unpaved roads
- More conspicuous than a backpack so airlines are more likely to check the weight and size
- Most are too rigid to fit under bus seats
- You can't use it as a daypack

Some people would also say that suitcases are better organised and it's easier to access your stuff. While this is true compared to traditional hiking backpacks, travel backpacks open along the entire front, giving you easy access to everything in your bag. Combined with the extra pockets backpacks usually have, they are just as easy to organise.

I travel with a backpack because it gives me a greater sense of freedom. With both hands free I can easily climb stairs, run for buses, and clamber on and off boats. I often travel to places where roads are unpaved with uneven ground that would make dragging a suitcase impractical. My backpack also works as a daypack, whereas a suitcase wouldn't.

Although most long-term travellers choose the convenience of a backpack over a suitcase, that doesn't mean you have to. In the Interview section and Appendix B, you'll find many travellers on extended trips with a carry-on suitcase. The most important thing is that you are comfortable—if you hate carrying a backpack or have back problems, take rolling luggage instead.

Lori Grant, who has been travelling with her husband since they retired (see their interview), says:

"We tried using traditional backpacks due to recommendations from other travellers. However, after a couple of long walks with them (shoulder and neck strain—ouch!), we found that we prefer using rolling carry-on bags instead."

Carry-On Backpack Requirements

I don't recommend a traditional hiking backpack in bright colours with straps dangling everywhere, unless you'll actually be hiking with it. You'll stand out more, the top-loading design makes it difficult to access your stuff, and the drawstring opening (instead of lockable zippers) means there's no way to lock it. Look for backpacks that are designed for travel rather than hiking.

These are the features I recommend for a carry-on backpack:

Carry-on size - It must meet airlines' carry-on bag limits (see the Airline Restrictions chapter). Around 40 litres is a good size, but anything in the 30-45 litre range can work—I had a 30-litre backpack for four and a half years. Travelling with a smaller bag is possible and will place you safely under airline size restrictions, but space is limited, especially if you're travelling to multiple climates. 40 litres gives you more flexibility.

Front-loading - Traditional backpacks open from the top and make it hard to access your stuff—you have to take everything out to get to the bottom. I recommend a backpack that opens along the entire front (also called panel-loading), like a suitcase. It's much easier to pack, keep things organised, and access your belongings without rummaging through everything.

Padded hip belt - A hip belt transfers the bag's weight onto your hips and off your back and shoulders. Simon's first backpack didn't have one, and he suffered from back pain because of it. Look for a padded hip belt that provides a good amount of support. Many carry-on backpacks do not include a hip belt or only have a thin strap that doesn't help to redistribute the weight. I consider it an essential feature unless your bag is very light or you won't be walking with it often.

Lockable zippers - Another advantage of front-loading backpacks is the ability to lock the main compartment and prevent opportunistic theft, as people can't easily grab anything in your bag. Look for a bag with double zippers that allows you to lock it using a small combination lock.

Durable - You don't want it falling apart when you're in the middle of nowhere—a quality backpack is difficult to replace in many places. A good bag will last years and is worth paying for.

Lightweight - As cabin baggage weight limits can be low, you don't want to waste your allowance on a heavy pack.

Simple design - This is a personal choice, but I prefer a plain backpack, ideally black, so it doesn't stand out too much.

Top and side handles - A sturdy carry handle on the top or side allows you to pick it up easily, get it down from overhead compartments on planes, or carry it like a briefcase. Padded handles are more comfortable.

Laptop sleeve (optional) - It's possible to manage without (my last backpack didn't have one), but a laptop sleeve is a good idea for added protection. For the best weight distribution, the laptop sleeve will be closest to your back.

Other things you might want to consider, although I don't find them essential:

Rain cover - Some backpacks have built-in rain covers. I used to carry a separate rain cover but didn't often use it. A cover can be handy to keep your backpack clean on dusty buses or dry if you're travelling in the rainy season.

Hideaway straps - Some bags allow you to pack away the backpack straps and convert the bag into a shoulder bag. This could be useful for business travel if you want a backpack most of the time, but need to look more professional on occasions. Our backpacks have this feature, but we never use it.

Compression straps - These straps on the outside of a backpack help to squeeze it into a smaller size. They are also useful for attaching items that won't fit inside such as a jacket or yoga mat.

Recommended Carry-On Backpacks

After over four years of full-time travel, we changed our backpacks in 2014. Simon was previously using the North Face Overhaul 40, which held up well through the years but doesn't have a hip belt, and he suffered back pain from wearing it. I had a Vango Transit 30 litre, which is no longer available, so I had to replace it when it tore. It's a small bag for permanent travel, and my overstuffing caused the damage.

On my search for new backpacks, I discovered that things have changed since we became digital nomads in 2010. Travelling with hand luggage has become more popular as airlines increase their rates for checked baggage, and there's now more choice of carry-on-size backpacks.

It was still a challenge to find the perfect backpack that met all of our requirements, but we're happy with our choices. Simon now travels with the Tortuga Backpack, whereas I chose the smaller Osprey Farpoint 40.

Tortuga Travel Backpack Review

Details

Dimensions (cm): 56 x 36 x 23
Dimensions (inches): 22 x 14 x 9
Volume: 44 litres
Weight: 1.66 kg (3.65 lb)
Colour: Black
Price: US $199 (Free US shipping)

Pros

The Tortuga is designed by travellers for travellers, and it shows. Fred Perrotta and Jeremy Michael Cohen created it after being disappointed with traditional backpacks while travelling around Europe. They set out to create their perfect backpack, and they thought of everything. It meets all our requirements.

Simon loves the Tortuga. It feels sturdy and durable. The padding on the back and hip belt makes it more comfortable and supportive than his last backpack, and he no longer feels back pain.

For a carry-on, it's spacious and easily fits all of Simon's stuff. The rectangular design maximises the amount you can take on a plane and makes it easy to pack, especially if you use packing cubes. ("Everything fits like Tetris," Simon says.)

You can organise your things with four pockets inside the main compartment, a large front pocket, two side pockets, and two in the hip belt, which you can reach while wearing the bag (useful for items like cash and phone when going through airport security).

The padded laptop sleeve holds laptops up to 17 inches and is at the back of the bag, close to your body for the best weight distribution. There's a separate zip here to access the laptop without opening the rest of the bag—useful at airport security. This does mean you need two locks for the bag.

A cover hides away the shoulder and hip straps, and you can then carry it by the padded top or side handles.

Tortuga offers free US shipping, and if it doesn't work out, return it unused within 30 days for a full refund. They pay for the return shipping on US orders.

The helpful Tortuga website has lots of photos and information about the backpack, and even packing tips on their blog.

Cons

The Tortuga sounded so perfect that I wanted it too, but it's too big for me. My previous bag was only 30 litres, so 44 litres is quite a jump, and it felt too bulky. They do make a smaller version, the Tortuga Air, but it's a bit too small (27 litres) and doesn't have a hip belt. Whether the Tortuga will fit you depends on the size of your torso—see their website for instructions on how to measure for it.

The backpack meets most airline hand luggage restrictions, but Ryanair is one of the strictest airlines, and the Tortuga is slightly over its 55 x 40 x 20 cm limit. It's only a few centimetres over though, and we flew with them without any problems.

If you put anything that's not slim in the front pocket, it bulks out and makes the bag look huge, so Simon doesn't use this pocket much.

The backpack is only available from the Tortuga website. If you live in Canada, Europe, Australia, or New Zealand, shipping costs $30-55. As we discovered getting it delivered to the UK, you'll also probably pay customs fees—we paid £35.95.

I highly recommend the Tortuga if you're looking for a maximum carry-on-size backpack. It's well designed, comfortable to carry, and has plenty of space.

The Tortuga Travel Backpack is available at TortugaBackpacks.com.

Osprey Farpoint 40 Travel Backpack Review

Details (S/M model)

Dimensions (cm): 51 x 33 x 23
Dimensions (inches): 20 x 13 x 9
Volume: 38 litres
Weight: 1.3 kg (2.87 lb)
Colour: Charcoal Grey (which I have), Mud Red, or Lagoon Blue
Price: US $160

Pros

It was a challenge to find a backpack smaller than the Tortuga that still met all my requirements, but the Osprey Farpoint 40 works well. Osprey is a well-respected company that makes quality luggage. They offer a lifetime guarantee saying they "will repair for any reason, free of charge, any damage or defect—whether it was purchased in 1974 or yesterday."

The Farpoint 40 comes in two sizes, S/M and M/L, making it easier to find the perfect fit. You should try both sizes as it depends on the length of your torso. I'm 5 feet 4 inches (162 cm) and the S/M fits me comfortably.

The backpack has two compartments: the spacious main one and the front one with a padded laptop sleeve for laptops up to 15 inches. You need to be careful not to overfill the main section otherwise the laptop compartment will be curved. Handily, you can lock both parts with one padlock.

Moving from 30 to 38 litres made a significant difference—the Farpoint has plenty of room for my belongings and is easier to pack.

There are two pockets inside the bag (one in each compartment) and a small zippered pocket on the front for easy access to non-valuable items. (It doesn't lock.) There are two mesh water bottle holders on the front.

The Farpoint 40's internal alloy frame provides excellent back support, and you can adjust the back for the perfect fit. Combined with the hip belt, it's comfortable and my load feels lighter. Although it isn't designed for hiking, Mirje from Anywhereism wore the Farpoint 40 on the Camino de Santiago and walked 10-25 km (6-15 miles) a day for 20 days with no problems.

You can hide away the shoulder and hip straps and use it with the provided strap as a shoulder bag. I never used this feature on my last backpack, so I got rid of the strap.

Cons

At first I didn't love the look of the Farpoint 40. I'd prefer black to grey, and the plastic zipper pulls look messy. It's still more neutral than most backpacks, and after over a year of use it doesn't bother me anymore.

The laptop sleeve is at the front, but for better weight distribution it's preferable to have it at the back, close to your body, like in the Tortuga. I haven't found this a problem as my Macbook Air is very light.

There aren't many internal pockets, but as I use packing cubes to organise my things, it's not an issue for me. The two internal pockets are quite large, so they are not ideal for small items.

Some people complain that the compression straps on the front of the bag go across the mesh water bottle holders, but I don't use them.

If you are looking for a carry-on backpack smaller than the Tortuga, the Osprey Farpoint 40 is an excellent option.

The Osprey Farpoint 40 is available on Amazon US, Amazon UK, and in outdoor stores like REI.

I don't think you can go wrong with the Tortuga or the Osprey Farpoint 40. They are both popular backpacks with other travellers; The Yoga Nomads and Till the Money Runs Out are couples with the same Tortuga/Farpoint combination as us (see their interviews in Part 4), and Jeff from Lengthy Travel and Mirje from Anywhereism travel with the Farpoint 40.

Other Carry-On Backpacks

The Tortuga and the Osprey Farpoint 40 were the only backpacks I found that completely met our requirements. There are many other carry-on-size travel backpacks such as the Minaal Carry On, Tom Bihn Aeronaut, and Goruck GR2, but these don't include padded hip belts, which we find essential to take the weight off our backs and shoulders. The REI Vagabond Tour 40 Pack is an option if you don't need a laptop sleeve and is cheaper than most of the others, but it's 1.5 inches longer than the carry-on restrictions, so it might not be allowed on planes.

The best way to find the right backpack for you is to try it on. You can always buy it, do a test pack, and if it doesn't work for you, return it. Outdoor shops like REI often offer free fitting services to help you find the perfect fit.

Carry-On Rolling Suitcase Requirements

If you decide you'd like your luggage with wheels, your choices are a suitcase, rolling duffel bag, or hybrid rolling backpack.

A hybrid backpack/suitcase may seem the best of both worlds, as you can choose to use the wheels or backpack straps depending on the situation, but there are downsides. The wheels make the backpack heavier, less comfortable, and take up storage space. If you use the wheels most of the time, you'll find it a hassle to convert it to backpack mode just to climb a staircase. While they work for some travellers, I think you are better off choosing either a backpack or a suitcase.

Here's what to look for in a rolling suitcase:

Carry-on size - This is even more important than for a backpack, as you can't compress a suitcase with rigid sides down for airlines with smaller allowances. Stick to a suitcase that measures 56 x 36 x 23 cm (22 x 14 x 9 inches) or less including all handles, side pockets, and wheels.

Two wheels - Four-wheel (spinner) suitcases have extra wheels that take up space and can break. While two-wheel suitcases tuck most of the wheels' diameter inside the bag, spinners leave the wheels dangling, taking up more of your carry-on bag's allowed length. Many travellers like four-wheel suitcases as they can be pulled alongside them, so they can be a good option if you'll only be using your suitcase on smooth floors. In general, two-wheel suitcases are more robust.

Strong wheels - Make sure they can manage rough terrain as you don't want your wheels coming off when you're trying to find your hotel.

Sturdy telescoping handle - This is one of the first things that can break. Aluminium will be sturdier than plastic.

Soft sided - While a hard shell case offers better protection, a soft case is lighter and easier to squeeze into small spaces.

Lockable zippers - To keep your gear secure.

Durable - It's worth paying for a quality suitcase that will last you years.

Lightweight - This is especially important in Europe, Asia, and Australia, where carry-on weight allowances are low. If your suitcase weighs too much, it won't leave you much allowance for your gear. You might consider a wheeled duffel bag, as they are lighter than suitcases.

Side handle - For when you need to carry it up stairs.

Laptop compartment (optional) - If you are travelling with a laptop and don't have a separate laptop bag.

Recommended Carry-On Rolling Suitcases

Aside from 10 days in Italy before we became nomadic, I haven't travelled with a carry-on suitcase. Here's what other travellers recommend:

Osprey Ozone 22" - Alex of Travel Fashion Girl loves this suitcase: "One of the most important features in wheeled luggage for me as a long-term traveller is ultra-durable rugged wheels I can drag through gravel, broken pavement, and up steps without worrying that my bag is going to fall apart. That's why I travel with this brand and not a regular wheeled suitcase with wheels that are made for smooth sidewalks." At 1.98 kg (4.37 lb), it's the lightest suitcase on this list, although still heavier than a backpack.

Pacsafe Toursafe AT21 - Nora from The Professional Hobo recommends this suitcase as it's "lightweight, sturdy, has nifty security features, and some handy organisational features on the inside."

Eagle Creek Morphus 22 - Jade of Our Oyster loves its versatility as it is two bags in one: "There is a section with wheels and another section that is a backpack which attaches to it. This means you can use it as one bag or separate the two and have two carry-on bags."

High Sierra 3-in-1 Wheeled Backpack - Shannon and Michael of Camera & Carry On say, "We love that it's lightweight, compact, and has a detachable backpack. While we use the wheels 99.9% of the time (even in the most remote places), there are two straps that can easily convert the bag for more off-roading scenarios."

Amy Magnusson of Permanent Tourist also recommends this bag although she says, "I thought I would use the backpack feature a lot more, but in Europe I only attempted it once and it didn't work well because it was too heavy and awkward. But if I had needed to run somewhere, I would have used it. The wheels were fine for that trip and all my other trips since then."

Travelpro Platinum Magna 22-inch - This is The Wirecutter's top pick for best carry-on luggage as "it has the best balance of size, price, reliability, and durable, high-end details." At 3.8 kg (8.4 lb), it's significantly heavier than the above options. The suit compartment indicates that it's more aimed at business travellers than adventurers.

If you are travelling long-term with a suitcase, I recommend looking at brands that target adventure travellers, as these are more likely to stand up to the rigours of the road. Osprey, Eagle Creek, and REI all have good options.

Carry-On Suitcase for Small Children

Sharon of Where's Sharon travels carry-on only with her two children aged three and five and highly recommends Trunki ride on suitcases for kids. They come in a range of fun designs, and kids can either pull it themselves or ride on it and be pulled. As well as storing all the children's clothes and toys, they work as a chair, and even a toy to keep kids entertained. Trunki suitcases come with a five-year guarantee, so they should be durable enough for long-term travel. They are recommended for kids aged three and up.

PART TWO

What to Pack

There are no rules for what to pack in your carry-on. It will depend on your trip. Will you be travelling in hot or cold climates (or both)? Will you be spending most of your time climbing mountains, chilling on beaches, or clubbing in cities? Are you on a round-the-world trip doing it all? There are ways to pack for multiple climates and activities, but you need to decide your priorities.

In the next few chapters, I offer suggestions for clothes, toiletries, electronics, miscellaneous items, money, and documents to pack. At the end of each section, I include my and Simon's current packing lists, so you can see exactly what we travel with. You can also find our complete packing list in Appendix A and links to lists from a range of travellers in Appendix B.

The advice I've given is adaptable, and you don't need to follow our lists exactly—replace skirts with shorts or jeans with leggings; leave the laptop behind and stock up on makeup; squeeze in four camera lenses if you need to. I provide a guideline of what's possible to fit in a carry-on, but this is your trip. It's important to pack what you feel comfortable with, and that meets the needs of your travel style and destination.

Deciding what to pack can be stressful, especially if you're travelling with hand luggage for the first time. Try not to obsess about the right thing to pack. There is no correct answer, and you can't screw things up too badly. Remember, if you leave something crucial behind, you can always buy it at your destination—other countries have stuff too. Ultimately, once you're exploring the world, you won't worry about what's in your backpack anymore.

5. Choosing Travel Clothes

The Perfect Travel Fabric

The ideal item of travel clothing is lightweight but durable, functional yet stylish, wrinkle-resistant, breathable, and quick drying, can be worn for hikes and nights out, and goes with all your other clothes. It's a tall order and most of our clothes don't meet all these criteria—although we have found some that do. The goal when choosing your travel wardrobe is to find items that meet as many of the criteria as possible, and that you feel comfortable and confident wearing.

Cotton is often advised against for travel as it isn't moisture wicking (moving sweat away from your body and keeping you dry) and takes longer to dry than synthetic fabrics. I like cotton and many of my clothes are made from it. It's soft, comfortable, breathable, inexpensive, and you can find it in any clothes shop. As long as the fabric is thin, I've found it dries fairly quickly. While cotton may not be the best choice for serious hiking, especially in cold and wet environments where quick drying and moisture wicking fabrics are important, for the average traveller it works fine.

Even better is a cotton blend that combines the comfort of cotton with performance fabrics like modal, polyester, and rayon. I've found these to be a good compromise as they are generally lighter and more quick drying than 100% cotton. Cotton blend clothes are inexpensive and easily found in regular shops.

The alternative to cotton is a technical fabric designed for outdoor activities such as nylon, polyester, or Coolmax. They are lightweight, quick drying, moisture wicking, wrinkle resistant, and durable. Some are even odour resistant so you can wear them more times without washing. The downsides are that technical fabrics are more expensive than cotton, designs are usually more sporty than stylish (with some exceptions), and they can be less breathable in warm weather.

If you are travelling to cold climates, technical fabrics can be invaluable as they maximise warmth in a small package. I always travel with a fleece, which is the lightest way to keep warm, and I've worn merino wool tops in colder countries (see the Icebreaker section below).

Another excellent travel fabric is Gore-Tex, which is waterproof and breathable and often used in hiking shoes and jackets. It can be pricey, but it's worth it if you'll be travelling in cold, wet climates—having dry feet makes hikes much more enjoyable.

Don't stress too much about finding the perfect travel clothes. There's no need to completely change your wardrobe; it's more important to pack what you feel comfortable in. If your trip involves adventure activities like multi-day hikes, you might need to take more technical clothing, but otherwise pack a few travel-specific items along with what you'd usually wear in the climates you'll be visiting, choosing items that meet the above criteria as much as possible.

I hear from many travellers, especially women, who regret filling their luggage with zip-off trousers and unflattering t-shirts and end up ditching them on the road. Kimberly York, who's on her first long-term trip in South America, says:

"I ended up swapping out a load of clothes because I bought new clothes before I went and didn't really like any of them. I was trying to copy a packing list I found online. I wish I had just bought my own stuff!"

Quality over Quantity

You have a limited wardrobe in your carry-on, so make sure you love everything you pack. I recommend buying quality items that last—they may seem expensive at first, but when you calculate the cost per wear, they can be better value than cheap clothing that will wear out quickly.

Some people travel with inexpensive or secondhand clothes as they know they'll get ruined eventually, but I'd rather postpone that for as long as possible. Although you can buy clothes everywhere, I don't enjoy shopping, and it can be difficult in places like Southeast Asia, where clothes are smaller, to find things that fit. My more expensive clothes last for years of constant wear and are worth the investment. The benefit of travelling with less is being able to afford to spend more on each item.

Colour Scheme

The common wisdom for packing light is to pick a neutral colour scheme for all your clothes. This is good advice as everything you pack does need to go together, but it's not strictly true. You don't have to dress in black and beige and brown if those aren't colours you like. Choose a colour scheme that suits you but only go colourful for either tops or bottoms. It's usually easier to choose neutral bottoms.

My colour scheme varies as I replace my clothes, but currently my three tops are shades of purple. These go with my beige linen trousers, blue jeans, and blue skirt. I also pack a few dresses that can be as brightly coloured and patterned as I like. My cardigan and fleece are black so they go with everything, and my shoes work with the colour scheme (beige ballet flats and purple sandals).

Simon has a similar method. His trousers and shorts are brown or grey, and his t-shirts and shirts are as bright as he wants. His fleece is black and his shoes are brown, so they work with all his outfits.

You could also reverse this and have colourful bottoms and neutral tops. Or stick with a neutral colour scheme and brighten outfits with accessories—a scarf, hat, shoes, or jewellery. The important thing is that it works for you. If you create your packing list to suit your tastes, you'll feel more yourself on your travels.

The one colour I avoid is white. It's a shame as it goes with everything and is cool in hot weather, but it gets dirty too quickly. I also do all my laundry in one load, and it's annoying having to wash one or two white items separately.

I also tend to avoid black, except for my outer layers and exercise clothes (it's more flattering!), as it absorbs sunlight and retains heat, which is uncomfortable in hot climates.

Covering Up

Be aware of the countries you plan to visit and whether there is an appropriate way to dress, especially for women. In many places local women dress conservatively, showing little flesh, and it is respectful to do the same. If you wear tiny shorts and tank tops in countries like India, you are not only being disrespectful of the local culture, but you'll attract stares, and even harassment, from local men.

You don't have to go to extremes, but my rule in these countries is to cover my shoulders and knees and not wear anything low cut or too tight. As I often visit conservative cultures, almost everything in my backpack meets these requirements so I'm never short of appropriate clothing. I usually wear loose trousers and tops and flowing skirts below the knee. In certain countries, especially in the Middle East, it's best for women to cover their arms and legs as well. If you are stuck, you can buy suitable clothes locally or cover up with a scarf.

In general, predominantly Muslim countries are the most conservative about dress. Countries I've visited where I cover up include India, Myanmar, Jordan, and Egypt, and in rural areas in many parts of Asia and Latin America such as Bolivia and Guatemala. If in doubt, see what the locals wear and follow suit.

Most churches and temples around the world (including in Europe) have a dress code for men and women. You'll likely need to cover your shoulders, thighs (no shorts), and maybe even your head (although I've found scarves are usually provided in these situations). If you are sightseeing in a tank top, bring a scarf or sarong to cover up when necessary.

On tourist beaches, it's usually fine to wear a bikini, although do cover up when you are walking around town. On the Muslim island of Langkawi in

Malaysia, I couldn't believe it when I saw a couple of girls walking down the main street in bikinis, right behind two women covered head to toe in burkas —you'd think they'd realise how inappropriate their dress was. At beaches, rivers, and lakes that are more off the beaten track, it might be best to swim in t-shirt and shorts if the local women don't wear swimsuits—they often swim fully clothed.

Men have more flexibility with their clothes, but taking your shirt off is inappropriate in most places, and in more conservative countries you might want to avoid shorts. It's unlikely you'd have any problems wearing them, but you'll fit in better if you wear what locals wear. You'll need to wear long trousers in most churches and temples.

Staying Fashionable on the Road

Travelling doesn't mean you have to throw your style out the window and start wearing hiking trousers. The answer to stylish travel is simple—follow the basic principles of mixing and matching clothes so you can transform 10 items into multiple outfits, but choose your normal clothes. Yes, you need to make sure the fabric is durable and lightweight, but there are plenty of options in regular clothes stores, and you may already have suitable items in your wardrobe. You can find stylish and practical travel clothes by brands like Icebreaker, PrAna, Athleta, Patagonia, and Anatomie.

Dresses are fantastic because they don't take up much space and can be casual or dressy. Leggings are versatile—wear them for exercise, to sleep in, under a dress in cooler weather, and under trousers when the temperature plummets. A pair of dark skinny jeans can be casual or dressed up for nights out. If you are travelling to cooler places, a blazer always looks smart.

Liven up your outfits with small, colourful accessories like a scarf or bold jewellery. A hat can transform your look—choose one then replace it locally when you want a change. Pick versatile shoes like a pair of attractive sandals or ballet flats that are comfortable for city walking but look great paired with a dress and a necklace on a night out.

Ultimately, style comes down to confidence—if you feel good in what you're wearing, you'll look good.

There are plenty of fashionable carry-on travellers. For inspiration see the blogs Travel Fashion Girl and Her Packing List and read the interviews with Alex and Lucy in Part 4.

The Controversial Issue of Jeans

Should you travel with jeans? I say yes.

It's a controversial issue, with many travellers advocating that you leave your jeans at home. They say they are heavy, bulky, and take ages to dry. This is true, but I think it's worth it in most circumstances. Jeans are comfortable, familiar, and you'll fit in better than in travel trousers. It's easy to dress them up (especially dark blue or black jeans) and when the temperature drops, you'll be grateful you have a pair. I live in mine when I'm in "cold" places (below 20ºC/68ºF) like Northern Europe and San Francisco in the summer, or in the highlands of Mexico or South America.

Jeans don't have to be heavy. In the summer you can find lightweight versions —avoid thick heavy jeans. Mine are a blend of cotton, rayon, polyester, and spandex. They are light, soft, quite stretchy, and don't take too long to dry. Skinny and slim-fit jeans will take up less space than bootcut styles. You could also consider jeggings, which look like jeans but are as light as leggings.

You can wear your jeans on travel days so you don't even have to carry them around. Simon doesn't do this as he prefers to wear his trousers with hidden zippered pockets for security. I wear mine on planes and in cooler climates, but sometimes it's too hot on travel days. I find there's plenty of space in my bag for them.

Although jeans take longer to dry than travel trousers, it hasn't been an issue for us. You don't need to wash them as often as other clothes, and when you do, find someone else to do it—we've never washed our jeans in the hotel sink. We use a laundry service (very cheap in many countries), take them to a laundrette, or use the washing machine in apartments we rent. If you have lightweight jeans and hang them to dry in the sun, they'll dry in a few hours.

The only situations where I wouldn't recommend jeans are if your entire trip is to a hot climate like Southeast Asia or if you will be mostly trekking or doing other outdoor activities. For everyone else, pack one pair, or if your trip is entirely to cold countries, a maximum of two.

Convertible Trousers: Convenience or Fashion Crime?

Along with jeans, convertible trousers are one of travel packing's biggest controversies. Some wouldn't be seen dead in them; others extoll their virtues.

There are definite advantages for travelling light—the trouser legs zip off to make shorts (or sometimes capris), so you get two items of clothing in one. This saves space in your luggage and comes in handy when the weather changes on a hike.

Personally, I'm not a fan of convertible trousers. I feel too much like a backpacker in them. That's fine for hiking in the mountains, but they're not versatile enough for cities too. I had a pair on our first round-the-world trip and, except for hiking in Nepal, rarely wore them. I felt frumpy when I did and found the synthetic fabric too hot in the tropics. I don't remember ever zipping off the legs to wear the shorts. Many women have told me that they also regretted packing them.

That said, some people love convertible trousers. They are worth considering if you are travelling ultra light, hiking often, or wearing shorts most of the time and only need trousers occasionally. For most travellers, the functionality gain doesn't make up for the style loss.

Technical Clothing Brands

Despite my reservations about travelling entirely with functional travel clothes, technical clothing has its place in the travel wardrobe, and companies are increasingly making clothes that are practical and stylish. Here are some brands you might want to consider:

Icebreaker

Icebreaker is a New Zealand company that makes clothes from merino wool. Wool doesn't sound like it would be great for travel, but this magic fabric really is. It keeps you warm in cold weather and cool in hot weather, and is soft, non-itchy, breathable, and lightweight. Best of all, it's odour resistant—you can wear it multiple times without washing it, even after serious sweating, and it doesn't smell.

Simon and I both took a long-sleeve Icebreaker top to South America. It helped keep us warm in cold weather without taking up much space. Although we don't find Icebreaker gear necessary in tropical weather, some travellers swear by their t-shirts as they are moisture wicking and dry quickly. Icebreaker also makes some attractive dresses and skirts.

Icebreaker gear is expensive, but it will last you a long time. I think it's worth the investment for cold climate and adventure travel. Ultra light travellers should also consider it, as it allows you to travel with less.

SmartWool

SmartWool also makes clothes from merino wool. Their socks are popular with travellers as they are quick drying and odour resistant. They come in many styles and thicknesses.

We took SmartWool medium crew hiking socks on a snowboarding trip to Finland and loved them. They were cosy and warm, fairly quick drying, and didn't smell. I wore them multiple days in a row (for testing purposes!) and was very impressed. They are ideal if you are travelling in cold weather or hiking.

Darn Tough

Darn Tough makes merino wool socks. I haven't tried them, but many travellers love them for hiking and say they are more durable than SmartWool —they even come with a lifetime guarantee.

Athleta

For two years I ran in a cotton tank top. It worked fine until I was training for my first half marathon and realised why runners don't recommend cotton—I needed moisture wicking clothes to make my 10-mile runs more comfortable. I ended up buying an Athleta Chi tank top, made from their Unstinkable fabric that never smells. It really works, even after a long, sweaty run, and it's perfect for travellers, whether you exercise or not. I also love the tank top because it's ultra soft, lightweight, and is longer at the back for extra coverage.

It's more expensive than a cotton tank top but less than half the price of a similar Icebreaker top.

Athleta doesn't just make fitness gear; they also sell stylish casual clothing—dresses, skirts, trousers—that is breathable, comfortable, and lightweight. Although not designed specifically for travel, some of their items are ideal. A friend loves their skorts (skirts with built-in shorts), which look like denim but are soft and light.

Athleta has a fantastic guarantee—you can return clothes if you don't like them, even after wearing them on a workout.

Lululemon

Lululemon is another popular brand specialising in athletic gear that looks good. Their clothes are primarily designed for yoga, but many female travellers love them for everyday wear.

ExOfficio

ExOfficio's Give-N-Go range is the most popular travel underwear. They boldly claim, "17 countries. 6 weeks. One pair of award-winning underwear. (Ok, maybe two.)"

While I wouldn't go that far, they are ideal for travel. They dry in a few hours so you don't need to pack as many pairs (just wash them in a sink). They are very lightweight, comfortable, breathable, moisture wicking, and odour resistant. They are more expensive than regular underwear, but you'll need fewer pairs, and they last a long time. Jenny Krones says, "I have been travelling with the same five pairs for four years, and it is nuts how durable they are!"

At the moment we only have one pair each, but when we need to quickly wash some underwear, we turn to our ExOfficio. ExOfficio underwear is available for men and women in various styles.

If ExOfficio doesn't work for you (or you don't want to pay the high price), you can find travel-friendly underwear in many shops—just make sure it's lightweight and dries quickly. Snarky Nomad claims that Uniqlo Airism boxer briefs made from microfibre are superior to ExOfficio and are half the price.

REI

The travel superstore REI sells a wide selection of outdoor and travel clothes and gear. If you're in the US, it's a good first stop for travel shopping as you'll find everything you need. I bought my backpack there, and Simon used to wear REI travel trousers until he switched to a smarter pair of Bluffs (see review below). It stocks many of the brands I've written about.

REI offers a 100% satisfaction guarantee, where you can return any product within a year if you aren't happy with it, and a longer warranty for manufacturer defects. Our friend's REI backpack clip broke after over a year of use, and she was given store credit for the full cost to buy a new bag of her choice.

The North Face

The North Face makes quality technical clothes and gear. Many items are ideal for travel, and their cold weather gear is highly rated for its excellent warmth to weight ratio.

I have a North Face fleece, Simon has worn their trousers in the past, and we've both bought hiking shoes and sandals from them that were durable, comfortable, and reasonably light. Their gear is pricey, but it does last a long time.

Bluff Works

Finding the right trousers for travel is tough. Most travel trousers are ugly, while normal pairs can be too heavy. Simon has worn technical travel trousers from companies like The North Face and REI that are functional but not exactly attractive.

Then he discovered Bluffs. Bluff Works was founded by Stefan Loble, who ran a Kickstarter campaign to create his dream trousers—smart enough for the office but practical enough for hiking, no ironing required, and can be worn multiple days without washing. They sounded perfect for travel, combining the performance of technical travel clothing with a smart look.

Simon has had his Bluffs for two years now, and he soon got rid of his REI travel trousers—the Bluffs have most of their benefits but look better. They are lightweight, comfortable, almost wrinkle-free, and have hidden zippered pockets to keep his phone or wallet secure. He has worn them on long bus journeys, horse riding, hiking, city sightseeing, to fancy restaurants, and even to a wedding. They've worked well for every occasion and still look as good as new.

He struggles to find trousers that fit his skinny waist, but Bluffs come in a 28-inch waist, and in one-inch increments, so he could get his perfect fit.

The only downside to Bluffs is the slightly rough fabric, which feels itchy and hot when worn in humid places with temperatures over 30ºC (86ºF). He usually wears shorts then anyway.

Simon has the original Bluffs, but he is looking forward to trying their new chinos, which are soft, stretchy, and wrinkle-free, with a contemporary look and the same zippered pockets.

Bluffs are the most versatile travel trousers we've found for men. (Unfortunately they don't make women's trousers.) If you want to travel with just one pair of trousers or are looking for a smarter alternative to hiking trousers, Bluffs are ideal.

Other Technical Clothing Brands

You can find many more technical clothing brands, such as Patagonia, Rohan, and Columbia, in outdoor and travel stores. There is an increasing number of companies making stylish clothes using technical fabrics. Their ranges are more limited and prices are high, but if you want to look fashionable on the road it's worth looking into Outlier, Nau, Outerboro, Ministry of Supply, and Anatomie (women only).

Tieks Ballet Flats Review

Ballet flats are a versatile travel shoe, but the cheap pairs I used to wear didn't last long given the rugged conditions I wear them in. With every new pair I suffered a painful break-in period where the shoes rubbed my feet so much they bled.

That changed when I discovered Tieks by Gavrieli. These aren't just any ballet flats—they are Oprah's favourite ballet flats. These quality designer shoes are ultra comfortable and fold in half so they can be packed easily.

I started with a pair of purple matte leather Tieks, which I loved, and now wear vegan Brentwoods in neutral beige. The vegan shoes are made from fabric, so they are lighter and more breathable in hot weather but not as practical in the rain.

Tieks Pros

- **No break-in period** – They are the only pair of ballet flats I've ever worn that have fit me perfectly right away—no blisters, no cuts.
- **Super comfortable** – All my previous flats had flimsy soles that make walking on cobbled and unpaved streets painful. Tieks have cushioned non-skid rubber soles (in their signature turquoise) that feel bouncy and have stood up to dirt paths in Thailand, a vineyard hike in California, and many hours on cobbled streets in Italy. I can wear them all day long and my feet feel fine.
- **Portable** – They fold in half and are compressed in a compact pouch, so they take up less room in my bag.
- **Attractive** – My Tieks are ideal when I want a smarter shoe than my sandals. (I often wear them for city exploring and out to dinner.) They come in an astounding number of colours and prints, so you are sure to find a pair to suit your taste.
- **Durable** – Despite being folded up constantly, stuffed in my bag, and worn in all kinds of situations, my Tieks are still going strong after 18 months.
- **Exchange for free** - If you are unsure about the size, you can exchange them for free and keep both pairs while you decide which fits best. I found going up a size was more comfortable.

Tieks Cons

- **Expensive** – Prices start from US $175.
- **Scuffing** – After a few months of wearing the matte leather Tieks, the toes and heels were scuffed. This may be because of the way I walk or

that I wear them on rough roads. After a year, I contacted customer services to see if there was a way to repair them; they offered to send me a new pair free of charge—impressive customer service! I replaced them with vegan fabric Tieks, which don't have the same problem. I was also told that the patent leather designs are less likely to scuff.

- **International shipping fees** – Delivery is only free within the US; they ship internationally for a fee.

After two and a half years of travelling on four continents with my Tieks, I wouldn't be without them. They are pricey, but as I own so little, I value quality over quantity, and I think having a well-made pair of shoes ideal for travel is worth it.

Tieks are only available online at Tieks.com.

My Experiment with Minimalist Running Shoes

Barefoot-style running was made popular by Christopher McDougall's book *Born to Run*, and proponents say it's a more natural way to run that puts less pressure on your joints. Minimalist or barefoot running shoes seem like they would be ideal for the travelling runner, or even those looking for a lightweight walking shoe. Unlike traditional running shoes, they have minimal sole cushioning, so they are very light and flatten to take up little space in your bag. They can usually be worn without socks—ideal for hot climates—and are machine washable.

The most famous barefoot running shoes are Vibram Five Fingers. Some travellers love these, but I'm not a fan of their unusual glove-like design. I decided to try minimalist running shoes that look like regular running shoes but have less cushioning. I started with a pair of Merrell Road Glove Dash 2 and initially loved how light and breathable they were, and they worked well on light hikes.

The challenge was running. I underestimated how slow the transition to minimalist shoes would be. My first short run left me with very painful calves, and I had to travel with two pairs of running shoes while I gradually increased my mileage in the Road Gloves. After many months I could manage short runs without aches, but long runs were impossible.

I didn't want to give up on minimalist running shoes as they are so practical for travel, so I tried the Merrell Mix Master Glide 2, which are still lightweight but have more cushioning than the Road Gloves. I was able to run longer distances but ended up with painful shin splints that kept getting worse.

Ten months after it started, my experiment with minimalist running shoes was over. The transition was too slow and the injury risk was not worth it. I went to a specialist running shop for a fitting and walked out with a pair of neutral, cushioned Asics Cumulus 17. They may not be as small or light as my minimalist shoes, but they feel much more comfortable to run in and my shin pain vanished.

There's no right answer to whether minimalist or conventional running shoes are better—you have to discover what works for you. If you do try minimalist shoes for running, be careful as it's not something to rush into. The transition takes patience and ideally you'll start before you travel so that you can alternate with your existing shoes.

Minimalist Shoes for Non-Runners

Minimalist shoes can be great for travellers who don't run but want a lightweight pair of trainers or sandals for short hikes and city walks. Getting used to walking in them will be an easier transition than running, but you should still start slowly and try them before you travel.

Minimalist shoes that travellers recommend include New Balance Minimus Zero; Vivobarefoot and Lems, who make stylish as well as athletic shoes; and Xero Shoes and Luna Sandals, who make barefoot-style sandals.

Where to Buy Your Travel Clothes and Gear

I buy most of my clothes from normal clothes shops. I am a big fan of White Stuff in the UK, especially their dresses, as they are colourful, made from lightweight cotton, and not too skimpy. It comes down to personal taste, so look in the places you usually shop for comfortable, lightweight, breathable fabrics. Simon buys inexpensive t-shirts from H&M and Urban Outfitters. Brands like Gap, Old Navy, American Apparel, and Uniqlo are popular with many travellers.

Some people buy their clothes on the road, which can save you money if you are travelling to inexpensive countries. Unless I really need something, I wait until we're visiting the UK or the US. I'm not a shopping fan and find it easier when I know where to go and what size to buy.

We buy certain specialist items from outdoor gear stores. REI in the US is a mecca for travellers with a huge range of travel clothes and gear. Mountain Equipment Co-op (MEC) is its equivalent in Canada. We often shop at The North Face and, in the UK, Nomad Travel, Blacks, and Millets.

We purchase some items online (usually when we're visiting the US) from companies that create niche products ideal for travel, including Tortuga Backpacks, Bluff Works trousers, and Tieks ballet flats. We often buy gear online from Amazon, which has a large selection and often the best prices. Zalando is a good website for buying shoes as they offer fast and free shipping and returns. When I only had a few days before my Finland trip, I ordered three pairs of winter boots (at discount prices) and returned the two I didn't like—a simple process.

Before buying, I read reviews on the product page and on blogs (see the websites listed in Appendix B for gear reviews).

Going Ultra Light

It might not seem like it if carry-on travel is a new concept to you, but we travel with a relatively large amount of clothes, more than we truly need. As travel is a permanent lifestyle for us, we've added extra items since we began in 2010, and these are luxuries rather than necessities. It's nice to have a week's supply of underwear and a few extra tops, but we managed for years without them.

If you are up for a challenge, consider travelling ultra light. Limit your underwear and t-shirts to three—wear one, wash one, and one spare. Take one pair of trousers and one pair of shorts or a skirt. Don't pack spare shoes, except maybe a pair of flip-flops. Add one outer layer, and you're good to go in many situations.

You'll need to do laundry more often (although odour resistant fabrics like merino wool help reduce the need), but the benefits are an even lighter bag, less stress, and more freedom. You'll be able to comfortably explore a city with your bag before you check into a hotel or head off on a long hike with all your belongings.

Many people travel this way—some even travel without any luggage at all! (See Appendix B for packing lists from ultra light and no-luggage travellers.)

6. Women's Clothes

These recommendations of clothes to pack for women are based on what I have been travelling with for the last six years. The list includes the clothes you'll wear on travel days, so not everything will be packed in your luggage. These are just suggestions. Feel free to substitute different items that suit your personal style.

3 Bottoms (jeans, trousers, leggings, skirts, or shorts)

- **Lightweight jeans** - For colder weather and cities.
- **Loose linen trousers** - For hot weather and hiking. I tried travel trousers but found them ugly and uncomfortable in hot weather. I now buy regular summer trousers in cotton or linen, usually from M&S in the UK. These wouldn't be practical for multi-day hikes or cold weather, but they work for day hikes and feel cool in hot weather. They protect my legs from mosquito bites on nights in the tropics. Although linen wrinkles, I'm not too fussy about it and find the wrinkles drop out once I've hung them up or worn them for a few hours.
- **Skirt** - For hot weather. I make sure my skirts are knee-length for when we visit conservative areas (see the Covering Up section). I prefer thin cotton fabric that feels cool and folds up small.

If I were only travelling in hot climates, I would leave the jeans behind, as I did on our first round-the-world trip. For cold weather trips, I would skip the skirt and replace the linen trousers with another pair of jeans or warmer trousers. If you prefer shorts to skirts or leggings to trousers, modify this list to suit you.

0-3 Dresses

In hot weather—where we spend most of our time—I'm most comfortable and cool in a summer dress, so I always travel with at least two (more recently, three). I like thin cotton dresses and make sure that at least one is knee-length and covers my shoulders.

Dresses are versatile—they work for nights out, beaches, and city exploring. In cooler climates, layer them over skinny jeans or leggings and you've got an extra top.

As stand-alone items they can add a splash of colour to your wardrobe, as they don't need to match your bottoms (unless you'll be layering). I like brightly coloured and patterned dresses; many fashionable travellers swear by the little black dress.

If you don't like dresses, leave them out and add a few extra tops.

3-5 Short-Sleeve Tops (t-shirts and tank tops)

I travel with three tops. If you skip the dress, you could increase this to four or five. Choose whatever style you prefer, as long as they go with all your bottoms. I like short-sleeve tops in cotton or cotton blends that cover my shoulders and are more fitted than t-shirts but not too tight. I try to find tops that are reasonably smart but comfortable in hot weather and on hikes. Technical t-shirts look too sporty for my taste, but if you'll be doing a lot of hiking, they are worth considering.

If you will be spending most of your time in colder weather, replace one or two of these with long-sleeve tops.

1 Cardigan

I have a long-sleeve cardigan in black so that it goes with my other clothes.

1 Outer Layer (fleece, sweater, or blazer)

I always travel with a lightweight micro fleece that maximises warmth in a small package. It's black, so it goes with all my clothes and doesn't stand out too much. It has a hood and pockets to keep my head and hands warm—I don't need to buy a hat or gloves unless we're in cold weather for longer periods.

If you are only travelling to a hot climate, you could manage without a fleece, but I feel the cold and often need it on planes, on air-conditioned buses, in cinemas, and in mountainous areas when temperatures drop at night.

I find a fleece the most comfortable and light warm layer, but you could pack something smarter like a blazer.

0-2 Workout Outfits

For the first few years of my travels, I didn't worry much about exercise. I walked a lot, swam when I could, and occasionally used a gym or did floor exercises. Then I started running on a beach in Mexico and was hooked. I ran my first 10k race in Thailand and first half marathon in California.

Initially, I wore board shorts and a cotton tank top that I'd packed as beachwear. They worked fine until I began to do longer runs and needed moisture wicking running clothes. I also began taking yoga classes and bought clothes for that. I'd love to manage with one workout outfit, but I often run and do yoga on the same day, so need a separate set of clothes. It has increased the amount of clothes I carry, but it all fits in my bag and is worth it for me.

I have separated my sports clothes from my main packing list, rather than adding them to my tops and bottoms above, because not everyone needs them. Whether you take exercise clothes is up to you, but be realistic about whether you are going to use them. If you're not sure, don't pack anything extra, but make sure your normal clothes include something you could wear —a t-shirt and shorts or leggings—in case the mood strikes. You don't need technical gear unless you'll be using it extensively.

Here are the running and yoga clothes I travel with:

- **2 tank tops** - For yoga I have a cheap cotton tank top from H&M; for running I wear an Athleta Chi tank made with their Unstinkable fabric (see my review in Choosing Travel Clothes).
- **Capri leggings** - I have Athleta Be Free Knicker, capri leggings that come below the knee and are also made from Unstinkable fabric. They are soft, comfortable, durable, and have three pockets. I wear these for yoga and for running in cooler climates. They are a little heavy for travel and take a while to dry, but the quality is worth it.
- **Running shorts** - In hot weather, I run in Brooks Sherpa 6-inch shorts. They have a back pocket that fits my iPhone 5 and two small front pockets for keys, money, and tissues.
- **2 sports bras** - I have a lightweight sports bra for yoga and a more supportive one for running. The first two sports bras I tried rubbed during long runs; I now wear a Victoria's Secret Incredible sports bra, which is the perfect fit. I would never have thought of Victoria's Secret for a sports bra, but my friend swears by them. The Incredible is a bit bulky, but the padding means it's supportive and comfortable, and the wicking lining keeps me dry.
- **Running underwear** - I used to run in my normal underwear; my Runderwear are a new addition. They are designed for runners and are seamless, breathable, moisture wicking, and chafe-free.
- **Running socks** - Moisture wicking socks help prevent blisters on long runs. As I mostly run in hot weather, I like thin, no-show socks.

When my running clothes didn't have pockets, I wore my money belt (see 12 - Documents and Money) behind me to store my iPhone (for tracking the run and listening to music), keys, tissues, and cash.

If I run on travel days, I store my sweaty clothes in a large zip-lock bag and wash them when I arrive at the next destination.

1 Swimsuit

Pack whatever swimwear you prefer. I have a tankini—bikini bottoms with a tank or halter top. A bikini would take up less space and can double as a bra, but I prefer being more covered up. If you are spending a lot of time at the beach, you could take an extra bikini.

4-7 Underwear

I managed with four pairs of underwear for years, so it's possible. In fact, three pairs would work—wear one, wash one, one spare. You can wash underwear in your hotel sink and leave them to dry overnight, or even take them in the shower with you to wash (see the Laundry section).

These days I prefer to pack a few extra pairs and do less washing. With seven pairs I can go a week before needing to do laundry.

I have one pair of ExOfficio travel underwear, and the rest are a far cheaper cotton blend from M&S that dry fairly quickly.

When choosing underwear, make sure it's comfortable, breathable, and quick drying. A lace trim is fine, but I recommend avoiding fully lacy underwear because it won't last long with all the hand washing and laundrettes it'll endure.

2 Bras

As with underwear, something simple, breathable, and durable is best. I avoid bras with heavy padding as they take up more space and feel too hot in tropical climates.

2-4 Socks

The number of pairs of socks you pack depends on whether you'll be spending more time in hot or cold climates. Two is enough for me as I don't wear them often. I bought my socks in a regular shop but looked for the lightest ones I could find. They are made from a polyamide and microfibre mix that is lighter and dries more quickly than cotton.

If you'll be wearing socks often—either travelling in cold climates or doing multi-day hikes—you'll want to pack more than two pairs and might consider SmartWool or Darn Tough socks (see the reviews in Choosing Travel Clothes).

2-3 Shoes

Shoes are heavy so it's best to stick to two pairs—one on your feet and the other in your luggage. I travelled with just hiking shoes and sports sandals for years, but I eventually wanted something dressier and added a pair of ballet flats.

The shoes you choose will depend on the climate you are travelling to and the activities you'll be doing.

Hiking or running shoes - Most people don't need hiking boots. They are heavy, bulky, and uncomfortable in hot weather. Lighter hiking shoes or trail runners are adequate for most hikes—I wore mine on a five-day trek in the Nepal Himalayas. Choose a pair with a Gore-Tex lining to keep your feet dry and in a neutral colour for a smarter look. I've owned North Face and Merrell hiking shoes. Both were comfortable and durable.

If you don't have plans for major hiking, take lighter trainers (sneakers) instead or any shoe that's comfortable enough for a day's sightseeing. As I run more than I hike, I switched to a pair of Asics running shoes. I experimented with minimalist running shoes, but they didn't work for me (see the previous chapter for the pros and cons).

If you are only travelling to hot climates, you could leave the heavy shoes behind and just take a pair of sandals.

Sandals - In hot weather, I wear my sandals most of the time. Some women prefer flip-flops, others pretty leather sandals, but I like robust sports sandals such as the ones made by The North Face, Merrell, Teva, Keen, and Chaco. The soles are solid and grippy for hiking on any terrain, they are comfortable enough to wear all day, and the waterproof models can be worn in the sea or on river crossings. They aren't the most attractive footwear (hence why I added a pair of flats), but it's worth the compromise for me.

My latest pair of Merrell Enokis are more attractive than most hiking sandals. They are less sturdy and have thinner straps than previous pairs I've owned, but the soles are rugged enough for rocky trails, and they're very comfortable. They meet all my needs from city exploring to warm weather hiking. Teva also makes walking sandals with a more feminine design.

If you'll be spending most of your time in cities and not doing adventure activities, choose any comfortable sandals or flip-flops you like; otherwise consider sports sandals.

Ballet flats - Flats are great travel shoes. They are small and light, go with everything, and work for casual and dressy occasions. I wear mine most of the time in cities and for nights out. I've been through many cheap pairs that hurt my feet and fell apart quickly; I now travel with quality Tieks (see my review in the previous chapter). Merrell, Ecco, and Cole Haan also make comfortable flats.

Sun Hat

Choose a foldable hat that you can pack easily.

Sunglasses and Travel Case

I store my sunglasses in a hard but lightweight travel case to protect them.

Cold Weather Extras

By layering them, the clothes listed below work for me down to temperatures of around 10°C (50°F)—and I'm sensitive to the cold. In the Cold Weather chapter, I suggest other items to pack if the climate will be even colder.

Erin's Clothes Packing List

- Jeans
- Linen trousers
- Skirt
- 3 dresses
- 3 short-sleeve tops
- Cardigan
- Fleece (The North Face)
- 2 tank tops (1 Athleta Chi tank and 1 H&M for running/yoga)
- Capri leggings (Athleta Be Free Knicker for running/yoga)
- Shorts (Brooks Sherpa 6-inch for running)
- 2 sports bras (1 Victoria's Secret Incredible)
- Runderwear running underwear

- Running socks
- Tankini swimsuit (PrAna Lahari)
- 7 underwear (1 ExOfficio)
- 2 bras
- 2 socks
- Running shoes (Asics Cumulus 17)
- Sports sandals (Merrell Enoki)
- Ballet flats (Brentwood vegan Tieks)
- Sun hat
- Sunglasses and travel case

7. Men's Clothes

These recommendations of clothes to pack for men are based on what Simon has been travelling with for the last six years. The list includes the clothes you'll be wearing on travel days, so not everything will be packed in your luggage. These are just suggestions—feel free to substitute different items that suit your preferences.

3 Bottoms (jeans, trousers, or shorts)

- **Jeans** - Choose a lightweight pair.
- **Bluffs trousers** - Practical but smart. (See the review in Choosing Travel Clothes.)
- **Shorts** - Technical fabrics work best.

Simon travels with three bottoms but could manage with two. If we were only travelling in hot climates, he would leave the jeans behind, as he did on our first round-the-world trip. In cold climates, he'd skip the shorts.

Travel Trouser and Shorts Requirements

Simon chooses jeans that are comfortable, reasonably smart, and not too heavy. For his travel trousers and shorts, which he wears on travel days, he has particular requirements:

- Lightweight
- Quick drying
- Hidden zippered pockets - To prevent pickpockets.
- Neutral colour - Brown, beige, or grey. Black absorbs the heat too much in tropical climates.

You can find travel trousers and shorts from companies such as The North Face, REI, Rohan, and Bluff Works. Clothing Arts makes pickpocket-proof trousers and shorts with many secure pockets. Simon hasn't tried them yet, but we've heard good things. Outlier's Slim Dungarees are popular for a modern look, but they don't have zippered pockets.

A few companies make all-purpose shorts suitable for swimming, workouts, and general wear. The All Over Shorts by Olivers Apparel have a casual look; Outlier's New Way Shorts are more tailored. Either could work if you only wear shorts occasionally.

3-5 Tops (t-shirts and shirts)

- 3 t-shirts
- 1 short-sleeve shirt
- 1 long-sleeve shirt

Simon originally travelled with three tops but added a few extras over the years. Along with t-shirts for casual wear, he has two collared, buttoned shirts for smarter occasions. He buys tops in lightweight fabrics from normal stores.

If you are only travelling to hot climates, you could leave out the long-sleeve shirt (although it can be useful as mosquito and sun protection). For cold climates, swap some of the short-sleeve tops for long sleeves.

0-1 Workout Outfit

Simon doesn't exercise often, so he wears one of his usual t-shirts and shorts when needed. If you'll be working out regularly (be honest with yourself), add an extra outfit.

1 Outer Layer (fleece, sweater, or blazer)

Simon packs a black, lightweight micro fleece that maximises warmth in a small package. You could choose something more stylish, like a blazer, if you prefer. If you'll only be travelling in hot countries, you could manage without an outer layer.

1 Swimming Shorts

4-7 Underwear

Simon started travelling with three pairs of underwear and has added more over the years to avoid having to wash them in the sink. Seven pairs allow him to go a week before doing laundry.

Choose lightweight, quick drying underwear. Simon has one pair of the popular ExOfficio underwear (see the review in Chapter 5). The rest are cheaper microskin trunks from M&S in the UK that he finds more comfortable, but they don't dry as quickly.

2-4 Socks

The number of socks you pack depends on whether you'll be spending more time in hot or cold climates. As with underwear, they need to dry quickly so you can wash them in the sink when needed. Cotton socks take ages to dry, so although Simon has travelled with them in the past, it's best to avoid them. He has two pairs of Bridgedale Coolmax liner socks, which are ideal for hot climates as they are lightweight, quick drying, and moisture wicking. SmartWool and Darn Tough socks are worth considering for hiking and cold weather (see Choosing Travel Clothes).

2 Shoes

Hiking shoes - It's tricky to find one pair of shoes that works for all situations. Simon looks for the most neutral hiking shoes he can find in plain black or brown. He loves his latest pair, the Scarpa Margarita GTX walking shoes, which are the smartest travel shoes he has owned. They have a simple design but with sturdy Vibram soles and a waterproof Gore-Tex lining for outdoor activities. They are attractive enough to wear to dinner, comfortable enough for a day's sightseeing, and rugged enough for hikes.

If you won't be hiking, replace the hiking shoes with any comfortable shoes or trainers (sneakers). If, like me, you run more than you hike, pack running shoes instead. You could save weight with minimalist running shoes, but be careful as it's a very slow transition (read about my experience in Chapter 5).

Sandals - In hot climates, Simon lives in sandals. He prefers sports sandals with rugged soles, preferably waterproof for water sports, river crossings, and rocky beach walks. He currently has a pair of Teva Terra Fi Lite but has bought them from The North Face and Merrell in the past. Other popular brands include Chaco and Keen. Flip-flops are a lighter alternative if you find them comfortable and won't be hiking.

If you won't be spending much time in hot weather, skip the sandals. You can always buy a pair of flip-flops anywhere in the world if necessary. Travelling with just the shoes on your feet is ideal, as shoes take up lots of weight and space in your bag. When we spent 10 days in Finland, Simon only had his Scarpa Margaritas—they worked for every situation and his bag was much lighter than usual.

Sticking to one pair of shoes and one pair of sandals is the best option for multi-climate travel, but if you want an attractive second pair of shoes, look at lightweight canvas boat shoes, espadrilles, or minimalist shoes. Vivobarefoot and Lems make stylish minimalist shoes that are very light. They could even work as your main pair of shoes if you won't be hiking or are used to the barefoot style.

Sun Hat

You need a hat that folds up and can be packed away. Simon hasn't found a foldable hat that he likes, so he doesn't travel with one. He sometimes buys a hat locally but inevitably forgets it or gets fed up carrying it around.

Sunglasses and Travel Case

Simon stores his sunglasses in a hard but lightweight travel case to protect them.

Cold Weather Extras

The items below work for Simon down to temperatures of around 10ºC (50ºF). If you'll be travelling in colder weather, read the next chapter for ideas of other items to pack.

Simon's Clothes Packing List

- Jeans (Levis 511)
- Trousers (Bluffs)
- Shorts (Craghoppers Kiwi)
- 3 t-shirts
- Short-sleeve shirt
- Long-sleeve shirt
- Fleece
- Swimming shorts
- 7 underwear (1 ExOfficio)
- 4 socks
- Hiking shoes (Scarpa Margarita GTX)
- Sandals (Teva Terra Fi Lite)
- Sunglasses and travel case

8. How to Pack for Cold Weather

One of the biggest concerns about travelling with a carry-on is how to pack for cold weather. It can be trickier than packing for a beach holiday, but there's no reason you can't pack light in the winter too. We've encountered snow in Argentina and Finland, and freezing temperatures at high altitudes in Bolivia, and we managed to stay warm with just the clothes in our carry-on.

Wear Layers

By packing layers, rather than one heavy jacket, you can adapt to changing weather conditions, and your luggage will be lighter. You can also wash your base layers more often—it's easier to wash a t-shirt than a sweater.

A good layer system is a t-shirt, a lightweight but warm long-sleeve top (merino wool is ideal), a fleece or sweater, and a packable down jacket (more on those below). If it's freezing, thermal leggings (long johns) can be worn under your trousers and for sleeping in. If you'll be hiking or expect heavy rain, add a lightweight waterproof jacket to wear over your down jacket. Make sure you pack thick socks, a warm hat, scarf, and gloves as these don't take up much space but make a big difference.

If you are only travelling in cold weather, you can break the rules and take a heavier jacket, as long as you wear it on travel days. One spring we travelled to Finland for 10 days and, as we started and finished in London, I was able to pack solely for that trip and leave extra items behind with family. I took along a knee-length wool coat. It's not packable, but as I wore it on travel days it didn't matter, and I liked having something more stylish for Helsinki. If I had been visiting multiple climates, I would have left it behind and managed with my down jacket.

Wear Your Heaviest Clothes on the Plane

As with any carry-on travel, wear your heaviest, bulkiest clothes and shoes on the plane to save space and weight in your luggage. In Finland, I wore my jeans, boots, fleece, and wool jacket on travel days. You can remove extra items on the plane and store them under your seat or on top of your bag in the overhead compartment—you could even take a tote bag for this. Stuff your gloves and hat in your jacket pockets.

Use Compression Bags or Packing Cubes to Organise Your Clothes

I always recommend compression bags or packing cubes to organise your clothes, but it's particularly important for cold weather travel to minimise their size. Bulky clothes like fleeces and sweaters work especially well with compression bags, which suck out excess air and will enable you to pack more.

(See 14 - How to Pack for more information on packing organisers.)

Take a Light, Packable Down Jacket

The secret to packing light in cold weather is a puffy, insulated jacket that is warm, ultra lightweight, and highly compressible.

Goose down has the highest warmth to weight ratio—it keeps you toasty in a tiny package. It stops being warm when wet and takes ages to dry, so you'll need to wear a rain jacket over it in very wet conditions. There are also ethical considerations, as feathers may be plucked from live birds. Patagonia and Mountain Hardwear use ethically sourced feathers, or choose a synthetic down jacket instead. Synthetic jackets aren't as warm or compressible, but they work better in wet weather.

Simon travelled to Finland with the Mountain Hardwear Ghost Whisperer, the world's lightest full-featured down jacket with 800 fill power, which is about the best you can get. It is insanely light (only 219 g/7.7 oz) but kept Simon remarkably warm.

I went with the synthetic down Patagonia Nano Puff Hoody. It isn't as compressible or light as down (it's 292 g/10.3 oz), but the difference is minimal. Synthetic down is cheaper, and I didn't have to worry about the ethical issues of goose down.

Both are fantastic jackets that kept us surprisingly warm for their size. They have similar features—two external zippered pockets (my Patagonia also has an internal zippered pocket), hoods, and they stuff into one of their pockets, making them easy to pack.

Down jackets don't typically perform well in rain; many people wear a shell or waterproof jacket over the top. Both our jackets have a water repellant shell and are fine in light rain—and it often rained in Finland. They keep the wind out and are ideal for active pursuits like the snowboarding, hiking, and horse riding we did in Lapland. We also wore them on a rainy trip to Cornwall in the summer, and I didn't need a rain jacket. Simon found his jacket leaked water around the cuffs in heavy rain.

We chose hooded jackets. In Finland, we didn't use the hoods often as we had hats, but in the warmer but wetter English weather they were useful. If you want to pack ultra light, save a little space by choosing the versions without hoods. My jacket is silver and Simon's is green, but black would be a smarter colour choice. Both jackets come in a range of colours.

Down jacket brands include The North Face, Patagonia, MontBell, Marmot, Mountain Hardwear, Arcteryx, Yeti, and Uniqlo (which makes a budget down jacket). Unless you'll be experiencing arctic weather, look for jackets described as ultralight.

Jenny and Tom Krones (see their interview) recommend the Yeti jackets they bought in Germany:

"We call them our 'super jackets' or 'Star Trek jackets' because they are crazy small, light, and packable but are all we need to stay warm in the snow. We layer them under a small rain shell and over a light long-sleeve shirt and sometimes get too hot in the snow."

Down (and synthetic down) jackets are expensive, but they are worth it if you are travelling in the winter, as they are so warm and packable. Combined with other layers, they enable you to stay warm in freezing temperatures. They are perfect if you are travelling to multiple climates, as they can easily be stored in your luggage when not being worn.

Managing Multiple Climates

If you are travelling to both cold and hot countries, you might wonder how to pack everything you need in a carry-on. It is possible, and plenty of travellers do so (see the packing lists in Appendix B for inspiration).

We spent the first year of our travels in South America, where we encountered a freak snow storm in Argentina, freezing temperatures in Bolivia's altiplano, and the steamy heat of the Amazon jungle. Despite the extreme temperature changes, our packing list was similar to our current one. We had a few extra layers and bought warm accessories when we hit the cold weather, but everything else was the same.

Start with the Basics

We always travel with the essentials—shoes, socks, jeans, and a fleece—so if we unexpectedly hit cold weather, we'll be able to stay warm. Start with a few basic items and add to them when needed.

Choose Fabrics Carefully

If you'll be encountering cold weather early in your trip, pack extra layers in technical fabrics that are quick drying (so you can take less and wash them more) and have a high warmth to weight ratio. You want items that will keep you warm in a compact package. Down jackets, lightweight waterproof jackets, merino wool tops, and thermal leggings are ideal. Read the technical clothing section for recommended brands. Compression bags and packing cubes will reduce the bulk of your extra clothes.

Pack Multipurpose Clothing

Choose t-shirts you can wear in hot weather and use as a base layer in the cold. Pack a dress to wear on its own or pair with leggings and a cardigan when it gets cooler. Leggings can be used as workout gear, pyjamas, and layered under your trousers when needed.

Bridget Rule recommends a merino wool buff:

"They're much smaller and lighter than a scarf or beanie, but they can function as either (hence we have two each—one for our neck and one for our head). They're soft and super warm, machine washable, and dry really fast."

Buy or Rent It There

If you'll be travelling for long periods in hot weather, don't pack your winter gear—buy it when you arrive. If the first three months of your trip are in Southeast Asia, there's no point carrying a jacket for when you reach New Zealand.

We always manage to buy what we need when we hit cold weather. In northern Argentina, when the weather turned snowy, we picked up thick socks, hats, gloves, and an extra fleece inexpensively at a market. You can find cheap winter clothes in secondhand shops, markets, and discount clothing stores like Primark in the UK and Target in the US—ask locals where to shop.

We borrowed and bought extra gear for our Finland trip in the UK. This doesn't have to be expensive—a hat and gloves in the market cost £5 ($8), and warm winter boots were £17.50 ($28) online at Zalando. You can even sell it once you've finished with it. Brandon Quittem (see his interview) managed the transition from hot Southeast Asia to chilly Nepal by doing this:

"We spent a month trekking in Nepal and temperatures were below freezing for a week, so we picked up a couple of knockoff jackets and pants to keep us warm. We spent $80 to outfit our Annapurna trek and made $50 back by selling our used gear to other trekkers."

Renting clothes at your destination is often an option. We rented snowboarding clothes in Finland and New Zealand, and jackets for a trek in Nepal.

Once you've moved from cold to warm weather, don't keep lugging those sweaters and jacket around, unless you'll need them again soon. Post them home, donate to a charity shop, or sell/give them to other travellers instead.

Our Packing List for a 10-Day Trip to Finland

For our Finland trip, we packed for both outdoor adventures (snowboarding, hiking, horse riding) in Lapland and city life in stylish Helsinki. It was actually easier than usual, as we were only visiting one climate, and we had plenty of space left in our backpacks. Both our bags weighed 8.6 kg (19 lb), which is around the same as I usually have but a few kilos less than normal for Simon. This was slightly over the 8 kg (17.6 lb) carry-on limit of Finnair, but as usual, they didn't weigh our bags. They only allow one carry-on bag, without an extra personal item, so Simon packed our cotton shoulder bag in his backpack.

We experienced temperatures from 2-12°C (35-53°F), although the wind chill factor made it feel colder, and it often rained. Our layers and down jackets kept us warm, and we never felt like we lacked clothes. We could have managed even colder temperatures as we didn't wear all our layers.

This packing list includes everything we wore on the plane, so we didn't pack all this in our backpacks.

Erin's Clothes

- Jeans
- PrAna Halle trousers – Practical but decent-looking travel trousers made from a water resistant material so dirt wipes off easily.
- Thermal leggings – To wear under my trousers.
- 2 tank tops – To layer under my other tops. I didn't wear one of them.
- 3 short-sleeve tops
- Cardigan
- Icebreaker long-sleeve merino wool top
- Sweater – As this was a short trip, I bought a cotton sweater on sale. It isn't practical for long-term travel as it takes ages to dry. Merino wool or cashmere would be better.
- The North Face lightweight hooded fleece

- Patagonia Nano Puff Hoody Jacket
- Wool jacket
- Running outfit – Capri leggings, t-shirt, long-sleeve top, sports bra, running socks, fleece headband.
- 7 underwear (1 ExOfficio)
- 2 bras
- 7 socks (3 thick, 4 thin) – One pair were merino wool SmartWool medium hiking socks, which were warm and odour resistant.
- Gloves
- Woolly hat
- Scarf
- Sunglasses and travel case
- Winter Boots – I bought cheap but warm calf-length boots with a fleece lining (basically fake Uggs), which I wore every day. They aren't waterproof—I would have purchased better ones for a longer trip.
- Running shoes – I only wore these on runs and could have managed with just my boots if I hadn't been running.

Simon's Clothes

- Jeans
- Trousers (Bluffs)
- 3 t-shirts
- Long-sleeve shirt
- Icebreaker long-sleeve merino wool top
- Lightweight fleece
- Mountain Hardwear Ghost Whisperer Hooded Down Jacket
- 7 underwear (1 ExOfficio)
- 5 socks (2 thick, 3 thin) – One pair were SmartWool medium hiking socks.
- Gloves
- Woolly hat
- Scarf – He never wore it.
- Sunglasses and travel case
- Hiking shoes (Scarpa Margarita GTX)

9. Toiletries and Medication

The important thing to remember when packing toiletries in a carry-on is that your liquids need to be in containers of 100 ml (3.4 oz) or less and fit in one clear, resealable plastic bag with a maximum volume of one litre or one quart (see Airline Restrictions for more information).

This rule might send you into a panic. You're used to dozens of large bottles of toiletries at home—shampoo, conditioner, shower gel, moisturiser, facial cleanser, suncream, mouthwash, hair spray, makeup—and can't imagine how you'll live without them. It's really not that difficult, and there are many ways to manage the liquid restrictions.

Minimise: What Do You Really Need?

If you're used to a range of toiletries like the list above, you need to start by cutting out some items. What do you really need to travel with? Pare your list down to the essentials. Choose a small toiletry bag and only take what can fit inside it, including your zip-lock bag of liquids. In 14 - How to Pack, I discuss what to look for in a toiletry bag.

I've found there are many toiletries I can manage without. Since I began travelling, I stopped wearing makeup and haven't missed it. My beauty routine is minimal—soap (or just water) and sometimes moisturiser on my face; shampoo and sometimes conditioner on my hair. My life is simpler, my bag is lighter, and I feel just as good.

It's liberating to realise that you don't need so many products. You adapt to having less choice and find that spending time on beauty isn't a priority when you're exploring the world. No one cares if your hair is frizzy, and neither do you anymore—embrace it.

You don't need to go as minimal as me—there's no reason not to travel with makeup and facial cleanser if you want to—but do think carefully about what you pack, challenge your assumptions about what's a necessity, and give a simpler beauty regime a try.

Travel-size Containers

You can either buy toiletries in travel-size bottles—many pharmacies and supermarkets have travel sections—or buy empty reusable bottles of 100 ml (3.4 oz) or less (or save them from previous purchases) and fill these from your large bottles. GoToob squeezable travel tubes are popular but pricey, and there are many other options—look in REI, pharmacies, and on Amazon.

Take the smallest bottles you can. For products you use less frequently, a 50 ml or 2 oz bottle will be plenty. For short trips, even smaller containers could be sufficient.

Multipurpose Toiletries

Look for multipurpose toiletries and cosmetics. Do you need a separate moisturiser for face and body? When I'm in the UK, I pick up a tin of Steamcream, a natural, lightweight cream that works for face and body and comes in a travel friendly 75 ml (2.5 oz) tin.

Other toiletries with more than one use include: a combined shampoo and conditioner; BB cream as foundation and moisturiser; coconut oil as moisturiser, makeup remover, hair conditioner, and more; and Dr Bronner's magic liquid soap, which can be used for any cleaning task—hair, face, body, laundry, dishes, even teeth.

Go Solid

Choose solid toiletries where possible, and keep your zip-lock bag for the liquids you truly need.

Lush Shampoo Bars

Lush solid shampoo bars are my top tip for carry-on travel. They are small and light, work as shampoo and soap, smell lovely, get around liquid restrictions, are vegan and better for the environment (no packaging), and you don't have to worry about leaks like with liquid shampoos. They last ages —Lush claim one bar provides around 80 washes, the same as two or three 250 ml (8.5 oz) bottles of liquid shampoo.

To use a shampoo bar, wet your hair and the bar, rub it onto your scalp a few times, and massage it in until it foams like regular shampoo. Try to keep the bar dry after you've used it, and before you put it back in the tin, as it'll last longer. Lush bars also work well as body (and laundry) soap, but this uses them up faster, so we only use our bar when necessary.

You can buy shampoo bars from Lush shops in 48 countries—see their website to find your nearest one. There is a range of bars available, so choose one for your hair type or that smells the best! I recommend buying the reusable tin to store it in. They also sell solid conditioners, but these aren't as highly rated as the shampoo.

Solid Deodorant

I resisted natural deodorants for a long time because I assumed they wouldn't work well. Then in search of a good solid deodorant that is exempt from liquid rules, I tried Salt of the Earth deodorant, which is made from potassium alum, a natural mineral salt. The stick is solid, unscented, and dry. To apply it you either wet the stick or your armpits (which I find works best). This seems strange at first, and you need access to water to apply it, but I got used to it quickly.

It works amazingly well and keeps me odour-free all day, even after exercising and in hot climates. It's not an antiperspirant, so you will sweat, but this is natural and healthier for your body than chemical deodorants. It doesn't leave white marks on your clothes or residue on your skin—you don't even know it's there.

The 50 g travel size lasts ages—Simon and I have been sharing one for six months and there's more than half left. It lasts longer if you let it dry naturally (or wipe it with a towel or tissue) before putting the lid back on.

Other Solid Toiletries

Reduce your liquids by choosing soap instead of shower gel—it's smaller, lighter, and won't take up your liquid allowance. Most hotels provide soap, so we don't carry it with us and use our Lush bar if needed. If we're staying in one place for a few weeks or more, we'll treat ourselves to a bottle of shower gel.

There are many other solid toiletries available, including perfume, conditioner, facial cleanser, sunblock, and moisturiser. You can even try tooth powder or tabs instead of paste. Cloth makeup remover wipes are a better choice than a liquid cleanser.

If you are struggling to reduce your toiletries, solid alternatives are a must. The more you take in solid form, the more space you'll have in your zip-lock bag for the liquids you can't leave behind.

Long Lasting Toiletries

Look for toiletries where a little goes a long way, as your small bottles will last longer.

Guys, switch to shaving oil. Unlike shaving foam, oil comes in tiny bottles—a 15 ml (0.5 oz) bottle lasts Simon nine months shaving every two or three days. It's miracle stuff. Brands to look out for include King of Shaves and Somersets.

Once-a-day suncream only needs to be applied once and is water resistant, so you use much less. If you're spending the whole day at the beach, apply an extra time to be on the safe side, and don't dry yourself with a towel or you'll rub it off.

I like the Riemann P20 brand. It's an oil rather than a cream, so it's easy and quick to apply. I buy a 100 ml (3.4 oz) bottle every time we're in the UK and it lasts us months. When we run out, we buy normal suncream locally and transfer some to a small bottle before flights.

Buy It There

Remember that your toiletries only need to be under 100 ml (3.4 oz) on the plane—you can buy bigger bottles once you arrive. Don't waste weight and space by packing enough toiletries for your entire trip. Start with a small bottle and when you run out, replace it locally.

Most products are available everywhere. You might need to be flexible about the brand you use, although many big names are available globally. In developing countries, toiletries are sold in small sizes, so it's easy to find them in travel friendly containers. The US is most difficult as everything is jumbo-size, but I look for travel sections in drugstores like Walgreens or fill small bottles before flights.

We use a few items that aren't available everywhere such as Lush shampoo bars, P20 suncream, and shaving oil. They last us months, but when we run out we switch to normal alternatives or, if we have an address, ask our families to send us a parcel.

Contact Lens Solution

If you need contact lens solution, take multiple travel-size bottles to get started and buy more when you run out. Alison Garland from Travel Made Simple says:

"I've never had a problem finding contact solution abroad. From Europe to Southeast Asia, you'll find it. Look for optical shops—where they sell glasses, they will sell contact solution. A 60 ml bottle lasts me 5-6 days."

Makeup

Do You Need It?

In my previous life, I didn't wear much makeup, but I would never leave the house without at least a little—it felt wrong not to. While travelling around the world for a year, I stopped wearing makeup and never went back. It was freeing to break away from society's expectation that women must cover their imperfections (why don't men?) and embrace my natural look.

Your priorities change on the road. You realise that no one cares what you look like. You have a healthy natural glow from the sun and from living a life of adventure that beats any artificial cosmetic. And in the tropics, makeup melts anyway.

On a week-long trip to Paris, your beauty regime might not change, but most long-term travellers end up wearing less makeup than they used to. Steph from Twenty-Something Travel wrote about how she stopped wearing makeup on her year around the world—mainly because she was lazy and it was hot, but also because she felt released from cultural beauty rules. She still looks great in her travel photos and says, "My beauty secret was written all over my face: I looked so, so happy. Smiling eyes totally make up for a lack of eyeliner."

How to Travel with Makeup

Of course, you don't need to stop wearing makeup. Take it with you if it makes you feel good, but try to minimise by choosing a few key items that matter most to you.

Consider multipurpose cosmetics—Travel Fashion Girl recommends the Multiple makeup stick by Nars, which acts as blush, eye shadow, and lipstick; while Her Packing List likes BB cream as foundation, moisturiser, and suncream. (See Lucy and Alex's interviews in Part 4 for more ideas.)

To get around airline liquid rules, choose solid or powdered makeup where possible. For everything else, take the smallest bottle you need—look out for free samples in tiny containers or decant from a bigger bottle to a contact lens case or 15 ml (0.5 oz) travel bottles or tubs.

Hand Sanitiser

Being able to wash your hands without water or soap is often useful, especially in developing countries. I use hand sanitiser on hikes and long bus journeys, after using bathrooms that don't provide soap, and in countries with questionable cleanliness. Washing your hands before you eat is important to prevent transferring bacteria to your mouth and getting ill. Buy a small bottle as you only need a little and it lasts ages.

Mooncup: The Best Tampon Replacement

Ladies, if you haven't already switched to a Mooncup (or DivaCup), now is the time. It's a reusable silicone menstrual cup that takes up far less space in your bag than tampons or sanitary pads. In some countries it is difficult to find tampons, so using a Mooncup means one less thing to worry about. I find the Mooncup more practical for travel as it doesn't need to be changed as often as a tampon.

The Mooncup has other advantages whether you are travelling or not. It's better for the environment as it avoids waste—on average, one woman will use over 11,000 tampons or pads in her lifetime, which end up in a landfill or the sea. It's better for your body as it doesn't leave behind fibres or interfere with your moisture levels like tampons. It lasts for years (I've had mine for eight years), so although it seems a little expensive, it saves you money in the long run.

Menstrual cups do take practice, so try it out before you leave on your trip. Once I got used to it after a few days, I found it much more comfortable than a tampon—I don't even notice it's there.

Sharp Objects

You might worry that you can't pack certain beauty tools due to airline restrictions on sharp objects, but the rules aren't too strict. The only things you won't be able to take in your carry-on are scissors with pointed tips and blades longer than 10 cm/4 inches (or 6 cm/2.4 inches in some countries), straight razors, and safety razors (the old-fashioned kind where you remove the blade). We travel with tweezers, nail clippers, a sewing needle, and disposable razors (where you replace the cartridge), and all these are allowed on planes. You also shouldn't have a problem with small or round-ended scissors, nail files, and electric razors.

Share with Your Partner

If you are travelling as a couple, take advantage by sharing your toiletries. We have one toiletry bag between us and share everything except razors and toothbrushes. Toiletries are heavy—the less you have to carry, the better.

Our Toiletries List

- Toiletry bag (Lifeventure Ultralite Wash Holdall)
- Small zip-lock bag for liquids when flying (usually we fit our liquids into one bag between us)
- Suncream (100 ml Riemann P20)
- Lush shampoo bar + tin
- Toothbrush each + head cover
- Toothpaste (usually a 50 ml tube)
- Solid deodorant (Salt of the Earth 50 g)
- Lip balm (small solid tube)
- Hand sanitiser (50 ml bottle)
- Shaving oil (Simon, 15 ml bottle)
- Razor each + 2 or 3 spare blades
- Hairbrush (travel-size)
- Nail clippers
- Tweezers
- Mooncup (Erin)
- Hairbands and clips (Erin)

Sometimes I'll add these extra items in 50-100 ml (2-3 oz) bottles when needed:

- Moisturiser
- Hair conditioner
- Insect repellant

Medication

Keep It Minimal

You don't need a huge first aid kit unless you are heading to the middle of nowhere in rural Africa. Take a few items that are useful to have on hand, and buy anything else as you need it. Everything in our medical kit fits inside a small pouch around 15 x 10 cm (6 x 4 inches) and isn't usually full.

Prescription Medicines

When we're in the UK, we stock up on our prescription medicines (if you explain to your doctor you'll be travelling, you can usually get extras), but this doesn't last us until our next visit. Luckily, we've been able to find what we need almost everywhere in the world. Simon has migraine pills that can be hard to find, but we've managed to buy them in Thailand, Cambodia, Mexico, Spain, and Argentina.

Many countries require prescription medicine to be stored in its original packaging, along with a copy of the prescription. I've never done this—I remove pills from their boxes to save space, and keep a copy of the instructions—and have had no problems.

In many parts of the world, including Southeast Asia, the Indian Subcontinent, and Latin America, you can buy prescription medicines from pharmacies without a prescription. This includes antibiotics, the contraceptive pill, and many others. Make sure you know the generic name or active ingredients, not just the brand name, and it helps to write it down to avoid language issues.

If you are travelling as a couple, divide your prescription medicines between both your bags, in case one gets stolen.

If you have a prescription that can't be found abroad, you could ask someone to post it to you. Our friend's prescription pills are so bulky that she can only carry a three-month supply. A relative posts her more when she runs out. As she doesn't always have an address, she books a room at a large chain hotel (like the Hyatt or Marriott), gets in contact with the business centre to arrange the parcel delivery, and asks about the most reliable postage service in that country. She then picks up the package the day before the hotel reservation and cancels the room booking. It may be a little sneaky, but it doesn't hurt anyone, and it enables her to continue travelling despite her condition. Of course, if this bothers you, you could treat yourself to a night in the fancy hotel!

Contraception

The contraceptive pill has been available inexpensively everywhere we've travelled, although on two occasions I had to switch to Microgynon 30, which is the most widely available brand. The advantage of the pill is being able to skip a period by taking two packets back-to-back—very convenient if you'll be trekking to Machu Picchu or on a camel safari in Rajasthan.

Other travellers prefer long-term contraceptive methods like the IUD or implant, which can last three years or more. If you are considering changing your current method, you should discuss it with your doctor as far in advance as possible before you travel.

Condoms are available almost everywhere, so there's no need to pack a huge supply.

Our Medical List

- Ibuprofen
- Loperamide (Imodium) - For traveller's diarrhoea. If you have a bus to catch, you'll be grateful for these as they reduce your bathroom trips.
- Dimenhydrinate (Dramamine) - For motion sickness. I wouldn't be able to manage many of the bus rides and boat trips we do without them. They are prescription only in the UK, so I buy them abroad.
- Plasters (Band-Aids)
- Prescription medications
- Ciprofloxacin antibiotic - We sometimes have this on hand for severe cases of traveller's diarrhoea. In general, it's not a good idea to prescribe yourself antibiotics, but in practice, it's useful to have when you are without access to decent medical care.
- Antihistamine - Simon has allergies, so we sometimes carry these.

This is a good basic list. Feel free to adapt it depending on the illnesses you are prone to. Remember that you don't need to carry huge amounts of anything—unless you don't think you'll be able to find your prescription medication abroad—as you can buy more later.

Please note that I'm not a doctor and this advice is only based on my experiences. You should consult a doctor before you travel.

10. Electronics

We're digital nomads—we run our business online as we travel—and our electronics needs are higher than the average traveller's as we carry our portable office with us. Most people travel with some technology these days. It can make life easier, capture memories, and allow you to keep in touch with friends and family back home, as well as new friends you've met on the road.

For the carry-on traveller, technology saves space. A smartphone can take the place of a camera, notepad, book, guidebook, map, music player, alarm clock, calculator, and of course (and something I often forget), a phone. You don't want to get carried away with the technology you pack—take the least amount you can—but do consider how it could help you travel with less.

Some people don't want to travel with technology because they are worried about theft. I think if it serves a purpose and makes life easier, it's worth the risk. Accept it might get stolen and consider insurance. Read the Security chapter for tips on keeping your electronics safe—in six years I haven't had any problems.

In this chapter, you'll find a review of the electronics options. I am not advocating that you travel with all these devices—everyone's circumstances are different—but use this guide to decide what you need.

Travel with an Internet Device

Travelling with at least one device that enables you to connect to the internet —whether it's a laptop, tablet, or smartphone—has many advantages and just a few disadvantages.

Pros

1) Take Advantage of Free Wi-Fi

Most travellers these days use the internet for planning their trip: booking flights and accommodation, looking up bus times, reading restaurant reviews, and finding tips on travel blogs. Although you can do much of this ahead of time, it's likely you'll want to look something up on the road.

Internet cafes are becoming difficult to find and are often noisy, hot, and the computers slow. With your own device, you can take advantage of the free Wi-Fi found in many hotels and cafes and work in more pleasant surroundings—a balcony overlooking the sea or a peaceful garden. Even if your accommodation doesn't have Wi-Fi, you can write blog posts and emails offline and publish or send them when you find an internet connection.

2) Skype

Being able to talk to your family for free from anywhere in the world is amazing, and seeing them with video chat makes all the difference when you are travelling for a long time. Make sure your relatives are set up with a Skype account and know how to use it before you leave.

I also use Skype to call landlines. This isn't free but it's good value—£10 ($16) of credit lasts me a year or more. I use it to call my bank in the UK or to make local calls if I don't have a SIM card (more about using your phone abroad below).

3) TV and Movies

On long trips you'll appreciate being able to watch films and TV occasionally, especially after a stressful travel day or if you're ill and incapable of doing anything else. It's also useful to pass the time on long bus journeys or when the plane movie is dreadful.

I subscribe to the streaming service Netflix, which has many films and TV shows available on demand. The content differs depending on where you are, but by using a VPN (virtual private network—I use Witopia), I can access Netflix UK or US from anywhere. You can also use a VPN to access sites like Hulu, BBC iPlayer, and HBO GO.

A HDMI cable enables you to attach your laptop to TVs in hotel rooms and watch on the big screen.

4) Music and Podcasts

You can travel with your entire music collection on your laptop or smartphone and buy new music and download podcasts when needed. I wouldn't be able to endure long bus journeys without music or podcasts to keep me entertained.

5) Language Resources

Learning a few local phrases is necessary for most travel, and there are many apps that make it easier. I often download phrasebook apps to learn the basics, and Google Translate makes communication possible in 90 languages —I had an entire conversation with an Indonesian taxi driver using it.

If language study is a major part of your trip, using an online dictionary (I like WordReference) makes travelling with a thick foreign language dictionary unnecessary. Anki is an app I've used to organise my vocabulary learning—it uses spaced repetition to increase memorisation by repeating more often the words you don't know and gradually decreasing those that you do.

6) Online Banking

I do all my banking online. You could use an internet cafe for this, but your own device is more secure.

Cons

1) Space and Weight

While a smartphone saves weight by performing multiple functions, a tablet or especially a laptop will add weight and take up valuable space in your carry-on luggage.

2) Security

A device is one more thing to worry about: it's an expensive item that could make you a target. I take precautions to keep my gear safe (see the Security chapter) but I have to be prepared that it could get stolen.

3) Connection Overload

Hostels are less sociable these days as everyone is on their laptop or device rather than talking to each other. There's a danger of shutting yourself off from new people or local experiences by spending all your time on Facebook.

Many of us are constantly connected—texts, emails, and alerts flood our phones and laptops. Travelling with a laptop makes it easier to continue these habits on the road. If you leave it behind, it forces you to disconnect, to spend more time relaxing and paying attention to your surroundings.

Even though travelling with a laptop is essential for our work, Simon and I love to take digital detoxes from time to time—we escape somewhere without internet and leave our laptops behind (or locked in our bags). These have been some of our most memorable trips.

Smartphone, Tablet, or Laptop?

It's worth considering leaving your electronics behind for a short holiday, but for longer trips the convenience that an internet-enabled device provides is well worth it.

A smartphone enables you to take photos, plan your travels, keep in touch, find directions, and use helpful travel apps (see my recommendations below). A tablet gives you more flexibility, longer battery life, and a larger screen to make browsing easier. Many people use tablets for writing, ideally using a stand and keyboard. Memory card readers are available so you can transfer photos from your camera to a tablet.

If you'll be working, running a serious blog, or doing a lot of photography, then a smaller device won't cut it—pack a laptop. And if you're a couple who works online, take a laptop each. We thought we could share but only lasted a few weeks before we bought another one. You'll want to work at the same time so you can explore together.

For everyone else, leave the laptop behind and take a tablet instead, or for light use, just a smartphone.

Below I weigh the pros and cons of travelling with a laptop, tablet, and smartphone so you can decide which is right for you.

Laptop

Do You Need One?

If you are a serious photographer, writer, blogger, or work on the road, pack a laptop.

For everyone else, it depends. A laptop has many advantages, but you might be able to manage with a smartphone and/or tablet instead and save yourself the weight.

Pros

- Storing and editing photos is easier and you can use powerful software like Adobe Lightroom and Photoshop
- More power and speed
- More storage space
- Larger screen
- Easy backups by connecting an external hard drive
- More comfortable to write on a proper keyboard
- Better battery life than a smartphone (and possibly tablet)
- Best for working and creative pursuits like illustration or videography due to the larger screen, keyboard, and range of software.

Cons

- Higher cost than a tablet or phone

- Large and heavy - This is the main reason to avoid a laptop. If you don't need the power, a tablet is a better choice.

Which Laptop?

If you decide to take a laptop, choose the smallest, lightest model that has the power you need. Make sure it's robust enough to withstand the rigours of the road, the frequent movement, and hot, humid, and dusty environments. Good battery life is important to get you through long travel days and power cuts.

Simon switched from Windows to Mac just before we began travelling permanently, and I made the switch a few years later; neither of us has looked back. We find Macs easier to use, we waste less time on updates and virus concerns, and they are durable and light for travel. Some people complain that Macs aren't great for travel because it's harder to get them fixed in remote places. This may be true, but I believe Macs are less likely to break—the build quality is excellent, and in six years I haven't had a problem. Mac stores or resellers are found in many parts of the world, and the support from Apple is always superb.

MacBook Air

The MacBook Air is the ideal laptop for the carry-on traveller. It's fast, powerful, durable, has long battery life, and is unbelievably thin and light. It's a beautiful machine that's a pleasure to work on.

I have a MacBook Air 11-inch, which weighs just 1.08 kg (2.38 lb). I find it's plenty of screen space, even spending lots of time editing photos. It packs a lot of pixels into the small screen: 1366 x 768. It's surprisingly powerful for such a small laptop—I've had no problems running Adobe Photoshop and Lightroom and processing RAW images.

If you do need more space, the 13-inch version is also popular with travellers and still very light at 1.35 kg (2.96 lb). The 13-inch has longer battery life and an SD card slot, which is useful for photographers. (I connect my camera via USB cable.)

MacBook

In 2015, Apple released another travel friendly laptop, simply called the MacBook. It's even lighter and thinner than the MacBook Air and comes with a 12-inch Retina screen. It has some serious downsides though—less power than the Air, a less comfortable keyboard, and only one USB-C port that is used for all connections including power *and* USB. This means you can't charge your laptop and plug in your phone or hard drive at the same time. As it is only 160 g (0.35 lb) lighter than the MacBook Air 11-inch, it isn't worth it for me, but it could be a good travel laptop if the drawbacks don't concern you.

MacBook Pro

If you need more power than the MacBook Air, the MacBook Pro is an excellent option that maximises performance and minimises size.

Simon has a MacBook Pro 15-inch with Retina display. It's fast and powerful enough for almost anything—programming, video editing, and even gaming. The Retina screen is great for graphics and video work as you can fit more on your screen. If you're editing video, you can fit full 1080p HD video in your editor of choice and still have enough room to see all of your editing tools—impressive for something that can fit in your carry-on. Most people won't need a 15-inch screen—the 13 inch is more practical for travel, but for Simon's design work, he appreciates the extra space.

The MacBook Pro Retina is expensive, but when your laptop is essential to your business, it's worth buying the best you can afford. The main downside of the MacBook Pro, aside from the cost, is the weight—the 13-inch Retina Pro weighs 1.58 kg (3.48 lb), while the 13-inch Air is 1.35 kg (2.96 lb), and the 15-inch is 2.04 kg (4.49 lb). You won't find a lighter laptop with this much power though. The Wirecutter picked the MacBook Pro 15-inch as The Best Power Notebook, saying that "no other laptop measures up to the Retina MacBook Pro's combination of performance, keyboard, trackpad, screen quality, battery life, size and weight, and overall build quality."

Think carefully about what you'll be using your laptop for and whether you need the extra power of the Pro. For serious graphics work or video editing, you might need the Pro; otherwise the Air is a better choice for the carry-on traveller.

Windows Laptops

If you aren't convinced to go Mac, look for a Windows ultrabook, which is smaller and lighter than a regular laptop. Popular models include the Dell XPS 13, Acer Aspire S7, and Asus ZenBook UX305.

You could also consider a hybrid laptop/tablet, such as the Lenovo Yoga 900, Microsoft Surface Pro 3, and Asus Transformer Book T300 Chi, which combines the convenience of both devices.

The market is always changing so see sites like Too Many Adapters, The Wirecutter, CNET, and Engadget for reviews of the latest models.

Tablet

Do You Need One?

If you aren't travelling with a laptop, consider a tablet instead—it's small and light, and the bigger screen makes it better than a smartphone for surfing the web or watching movies. If you already have a laptop and smartphone, like we do, a tablet is a luxury item.

Pros

- **Small and light**
- **Cheaper than a laptop**
- **Larger screen and better battery life than a smartphone**
- **Watching films** - A tablet is more convenient than a laptop for watching films on planes and buses, and the screen is bigger than on a smartphone.
- **Drawing** - Combined with a stylus, a tablet becomes a digital sketchpad. The Apple Pencil takes this to the next level with the iPad Pro (see below).
- **Illustrated books** - I love my Kindle, but it's not ideal for coloured and illustrated books. Comics, guidebooks, and cookbooks work better on a tablet. There are also books that take advantage of the technology and incorporate video and interactive elements.

Cons

- **Storage** - You probably won't have as much space as on a laptop to store photos, movies, and music. You can't attach an external hard drive to create a backup.
- **Limited software** - Although software like Adobe Lightroom and other creative packages have iPad apps, they aren't as powerful as the laptop versions.
- **Size** - A tablet won't fit in your pocket, so it's not as convenient as a phone, and the screen is not as big as on a laptop for watching movies, etc.
- **Unwieldy as a camera** - Although most tablets have built-in cameras, they are awkward to use. A smartphone is a better camera replacement.
- **Typing is slow** - If you'll be typing a lot, buy a Bluetooth keyboard, which will be quicker than typing on the screen.
- **Managing photos is more difficult** - It's not as easy to store, edit, and back up photos as it is on a laptop, although it can be done.

Which Tablet?

As you can see, we're in the Apple family. We appreciate that they produce beautiful, quality items that just work and offer excellent customer service. This comes at a premium in price, but for us, it's worth it.

We used to travel with an iPad Mini, which is smaller and lighter than the iPad Air. We never wanted a bigger screen size and found it easier to hold. If a tablet is your primary device, you might appreciate the larger screen and extra power of the iPad Air.

The iPad Pro is the largest and most powerful iPad. For most people, it's probably overkill. Its real benefit is for artists and illustrators, as combined with the Apple Pencil, it becomes a high-quality digital sketchpad. The Pencil is sensitive to pressure and tilt, so it replicates a conventional pencil, but with pixel-perfect precision. Simon recently bought one and is loving it so far—he now does all his drawing digitally. He wishes it came in a smaller size (it's bigger than my laptop!), but it has replaced his iPad Mini, Wacom Bamboo graphics tablet, Moleskine notebook, sketchpad, and many pens and pencils. By using the Duet app, the iPad Pro also becomes a beautiful second monitor, and the Astropad app turns it into a professional-level graphics tablet.

If you'd prefer an Android tablet, highly rated options include the Samsung Galaxy Tab, Nvidia Shield, and Google Nexus.

Tablet Accessories

- **Case** - We use a neoprene sleeve.
- **Stand** - We have an ordinary plate stand. It's far cheaper and smaller than stands designed for the iPad and works well.
- **Apple Pencil** - For drawing on the iPad Pro. Any stylus works for drawing on other tablets.
- **Bluetooth Keyboard** - We don't use one, but if you aren't taking a laptop and plan to write more than the odd email, a keyboard will make writing easier. The Logitech Ultrathin iPad keyboard case is popular and also works as a case and stand.
- **Camera Connection Kit** - If you aren't travelling with a laptop, the iPad camera connection kit (or equivalent for Android tablets), will enable you to transfer photos onto your iPad from your camera memory card or via USB.

Smartphone

Do You Need One?

We travelled for three years without a phone, so no, you don't need one. In reality, most travellers do have a phone these days, and they are very convenient. We rarely use our iPhone as a phone, but having the internet in our pocket makes our life easier, especially for directions.

If you decide not to pack a laptop or tablet, it's worth taking a smartphone—even if you don't use it with a SIM card, you can get online wherever there's free Wi-Fi.

Pros

- **Small and light**
- **Multiple functions** - As well as being a phone, it replaces a watch, alarm, calculator, torch (flashlight), notebook, guidebook, music

player, and much more.

- **Camera** - Smartphone cameras are of such high quality that unless you are a serious photographer, you could leave your camera behind. You'll likely always have your phone with you (unlike heavy cameras), so you'll never miss a photo opportunity. I take many of my photos with our phone when I can't be bothered to take my camera out. It has other advantages over my camera too—I love the easy panoramic and HDR photos and slow-motion video.
- **Look up directions** - Being able to find hotels, restaurants, and sights has made our lives so much easier. Turn-by-turn spoken directions are helpful on road trips.
- **Huge array of apps**—There are many useful apps for travel. I use apps like Foursquare and Yelp to find nearby restaurants, Trail Wallet to track our expenses, language apps to translate menus, and a running app to see my running progress. I've listed more of my favourite apps below.
- **Tether** - This is an incredibly useful feature. Most smartphones can be turned into mobile hotspots so you can connect your other devices to it and share its internet connection. We often tether our laptops to our phone when the Wi-Fi goes down, in countries where the 3G is faster than the Wi-Fi, and when we're staying in places without Wi-Fi.
- **Communication** - You can use it to call and message people!

Cons

- **Battery life** - Most smartphone batteries won't last for more than a day. Tablets usually have much better battery life.
- **Small screen**
- **Typing is slow** - It's not the best choice if you plan to write a lot.
- **Easier to lose** - You need to be more careful with your phone, as it's easier to leave it behind or drop it down the toilet.
- **Connection overload** - Being constantly connected can prevent us from engaging in our surroundings, distracting us from the beautiful and unusual around us. I find it helps to turn off my notifications so that I only engage with the technology when I choose to, not when someone emails or tags me on Facebook.

Which Phone?

Basic Phone

If you're not travelling with a laptop or tablet, pack a smartphone to take advantage of the above benefits. If you are, you could pack a cheap phone just for making calls. I don't make enough phone calls to justify carrying a basic phone—the main things I use it for are the smartphone features.

Smartphone

I travel with an iPhone and don't think you can go wrong with that, but it's a personal choice and depends on which ecosystem you prefer. Android smartphones to consider include Samsung Galaxy and Google Nexus, or the Motorola Moto G for a budget option.

Make sure your phone is unlocked so you can buy local media—it's much cheaper (more on that below).

iPod Touch or MP3 Player

Even if you decide against travelling with a phone, consider an MP3 player for listening to music on long journeys. An iPod Touch is a good option if you don't need a phone but would like the other benefits of an iPhone at a lower price. Or choose a smaller, cheaper device if all you want is music.

How to Use a Mobile Phone Abroad

Using a mobile phone abroad can be very expensive. For short trips, you could manage with an international roaming plan from your home country. For long-term travellers, it's best to travel with an unlocked GSM phone and buy local SIM cards in each country you visit.

There are other options, such as international SIM cards that work in multiple countries, but these are expensive and only worth it if you are changing countries frequently.

How to Find Local SIM Cards and the Best Data Plans

Before we arrive in a country, I research which phone companies sell prepaid SIM cards and the data plans they offer. We use at least 1 GB of data a month, more in countries where the internet is unreliable, and we'll need to tether our laptops. Consult the websites Too Many Adapters, which has guides to buying SIMs in different countries, and Prepaid Data SIM Card Wiki. You can also search using terms like "best prepaid data plans in X" or "prepaid SIM in X." If there isn't much information online, ask expats or locals once you arrive, or visit a mobile phone shop.

If the phone company has a stand at the airport, this is the most convenient place to buy a SIM. If not, visit their shop when you arrive, or in many countries (especially in Southeast Asia), you can buy SIMs from convenience stores. Sometimes you need your passport. Even when Nano SIMs (which we need for our iPhones) aren't available, mobile shops can cut down full-size SIMs.

We've bought SIM cards in more than 12 countries, and the process is usually very simple. The cheapest country was Cambodia, where the SIM cost $2, and 3.5 GB of data was $5. The most expensive was the US, where the card was free, but 2 GB of data cost $60. In the UK, Three's Feel at Home service allows you to use your phone in nearly 20 countries at no extra cost. Although it's not designed for long-term use, we used it in five countries in a year. It meant we didn't have to bother buying a local SIM (especially useful on short trips), and it saved us money in the US, where data plans are expensive.

Recommended Apps

If you travel with a smartphone or tablet, here are some apps that I recommend. Most have iOS and Android versions—I've noted the apps that are iOS only.

Travel Planning and Booking

- **Skyscanner** - My favourite flight comparison tool. Choose "Everywhere" as your destination for inspiration on where to go next.
- **Skypicker** - Another flight comparison app that combines different airlines to find the best deals.
- **Airbnb** - Book apartments and rooms in people's homes. This is my favourite way to travel because whole apartments can be cheaper than hotel rooms.
- **Booking.com** - My favourite hotel booking app. It's easy to use, has

great deals, and they don't charge any extra fees.
- **TripAdvisor** - Hotel, restaurant, and activity reviews.
- **TripIt** - Organise your trip reservations in one place.
- **Uber** - The easiest way to call a taxi. You can request a car with one tap, and it arrives in minutes, costs less than a normal taxi, and is charged to your credit card.

Travel Finance

- **Trail Wallet** - An easy travel expense tracker. We built it for ourselves and still use it every day to help us stay on budget. It converts between over 200 currencies, and groups your spending by trip, month, and category. *iOS only.*
- **Currency** - A simple, gesture-based currency conversion app. *iOS only.*
- **XE Currency** - Not as attractive as Currency, but it's free and available for Android.

Navigation and Finding Businesses

- **Google Maps** - Although Apple's Maps app works well in some locations (such as the US), we find Google Maps more reliable in most places.
- **Foursquare** - Find nearby businesses and attractions. It often features places that the map apps don't have (or have in the wrong location) so is useful for navigation too.
- **Yelp** - Another way to find restaurants and shops. It works best in the US, although also has content for Canada, the UK, Australia, and parts of Europe. I love being able to type "vegetarian restaurant" or "sandwich" into the app and find the nearest places, along with reviews and menus.
- **Happy Cow** - For finding nearby vegetarian restaurants.

Writing, Reading, and Lists

- **Clear** - A list-making app that's a pleasure to use with colourful boxes to interact with. *iOS only.*
- **Byword** - A note-taking app for writing on the go. Simon pairs it with NVAlt on the desktop, which also syncs via Dropbox, so he can write

on the Mac and pick it up on the iPhone/iPad (or vice versa). *iOS only.*

- **Day One** - The ultimate journalling app with photos, tags, locations, weather, and markdown support, all wrapped up in a beautiful interface. *iOS only.*
- **Instapaper** - Save articles to read offline.
- **Kindle** - Buy books from the Amazon store and read them on your phone. It syncs across all devices, so you can start reading a book on your iPad and continue later on your iPhone.

Languages

- **Duolingo** - A free app that makes language learning fun and addictive.
- **Google Translate** - Translate 90 languages for free—a lifesaver when you need to look up a word or phrase when you're out and about. The camera feature is incredible—point your phone at a sign or menu and it instantly translates.
- **WordReference** - A more accurate dictionary than Google Translate, but it only works for single words and isn't available in as many languages.

Photography and Drawing

- **Instagram** - A fun way to share photos, with built-in filters and basic photo editing tools. Find us at @neverendingvoyage.
- **Pro HDR** - Take stunning HDR photos.
- **Snapseed** - Easy but effective photo editing.
- **Drawing Class** - Simon created this app to replicate a life drawing class with timed poses. *iOS only.*
- **Procreate** - A powerful drawing and painting app for the iPad. *iOS only.*
- **Astropad** - Turn your iPad into a drawing tablet for Mac. *iOS only.*

General Apps

- **Skype** - Call other Skype accounts for free or any phone number at reasonable rates. Useful for international calls that would be expensive using a local SIM card.

- **Touchnote** - Send real postcards using your photos.
- **Speedtest** - Check Wi-Fi speeds before committing to accommodation (or a coffee shop).
- **Overcast** - My favourite podcast app. *iOS only.*
- **iSmoothRun** - A comprehensive run tracking app that keeps me motivated. *iOS only.*
- **Forecast** - My go-to weather app. It's a web app, so you won't find it in the App Store. Go to forecast.io on your phone and add it to your home screen.
- **1Password** - Keep track of your passwords (we also use the Mac app).
- **Duet Display** - Turn your iPad into a second monitor for your laptop via USB. *iOS only.*
- **GarageBand** - A powerful, multitrack recording system with a range of high-quality virtual instruments. *iOS only.*

Apple Watch

The Apple Watch is by no means essential for travel, but some iPhone owners might consider it for a number of useful features. You need an iPhone to use it, as it works as an extension of your phone, showing your phone's notifications and performing simple tasks as a remote control.

Simon bought a 42 mm Apple Watch Sport as a curious iOS developer and technology geek. Most of the features are pure conveniences, but he feels they make a big impact. He loves not having to take out his phone to do small tasks—check the time, read messages, control music, look at maps, see the calendar, check a shopping list, call an Uber, even pay for a Pret A Manger sandwich! It makes life easier, is less conspicuous than taking out his phone, and helps him disconnect. While travelling with more technology might seem like it would have the opposite effect, Simon finds that he wastes less time on social media now that he takes out his phone less often.

The most significant impact the watch has had on Simon's life is to his health. He's a skinny guy who doesn't need to watch his weight, so he has never done much exercise. The watch changed that. It has an activity tracker that tracks your workouts, calories burned, and standing goal (it taps your wrist every hour to remind you to stand for a minute), and it shows the results on a circular progress indicator. It makes exercise a game and is very motivating. Simon doesn't like to ruin his streak of completed rings, so he will often be found doing press ups at 10 p.m. to burn his remaining calories. It also encourages us to walk more—an excellent way to explore a new place.

Finally, there's the joy I see on his face every time he talks into his watch to give Siri instructions to send a message, set a reminder, or look up directions. The future has arrived.

Smartwatches are in their early days, and their usefulness will depend on which features you'll take advantage of. Apps on the Apple Watch are still limited, and there's nothing on it that will improve your travel experience that your phone can't already do. It's also another expensive device to travel with and will be on display most of the time in hot countries, which could make you a target. That said, Simon loves his and so far (on our travels in Europe and Southeast Asia) has felt safe wearing it.

For Android users looking for a smartwatch, the Pebble Steel gets good reviews. If you are only interested in activity tracking, consider a Fitbit instead. It's cheaper and becoming more popular with travellers who want to stay healthy on the road.

E-Book Reader

Do You Need One?

For travellers who love to read, an e-book reader is essential. It saves an enormous amount of weight and space in your luggage and gives you access to thousands of books, not just the John Grisham novels in the hostel book collection. If you only read occasionally, you could use your smartphone or tablet instead, or just carry one book.

This pros and cons list applies to the Amazon Kindle Paperwhite, which is the most popular e-book reader, but other e-readers have many of the same features.

Pros

- **Small and light** - The Kindle is smaller than a paperback yet contains thousands of books.
- **Paper-like screen** - It uses an e-ink display which is just like paper.

There's no glare so you can read in bright sunlight.

- **Built-in light** - The light is handy in rooms without adequate lighting or when I want to read after Simon has gone to sleep. Perfect for hostels and bus or train journeys at night.
- **Easy to hold** - It's more comfortable than reading a paper book. As it's so light, you can easily hold it in one hand—ideal for snuggling in bed. To flip a page, simply tap or swipe the screen.
- **Long battery life** - The battery lasts up to eight weeks without Wi-Fi, much longer than a smartphone or tablet.
- **Choice of books** - Amazon has a massive range of digital books. There are many free classic books on Amazon and sites like Project Gutenberg, and you can subscribe to newspapers and magazines.
- **Easy to buy** - Amazon stores your credit card details, so you can buy books with one click from your Kindle or the Amazon website.
- **Sample chapters** - I love the ability to read a few chapters before I buy.
- **It's not just for books** - You can read PDFs, DOC, HTML, JPEG and TXT files on the Kindle. You need to convert them first, but this is easily done by emailing them to your Kindle email address, or using the free Calibre software.
- **Highlight and make notes** - As well as bookmarking pages, you can highlight words or passages and make notes.
- **Dictionary** - Tap a word and the definition appears on the screen. Each word is saved to the Vocabulary Builder file, where you can test yourself with flashcards.
- **Reading in foreign languages** - Tap a word or highlight a section to translate it into other languages. I bought a Spanish to English dictionary, which makes reading Spanish books much easier.
- **Sync across devices** - If you have the free Kindle app, when you buy a book, it downloads to all your registered devices and even saves your page.
- **Read blog posts** - I use Instapaper, a free tool for saving web pages to read later.

Cons

- **Guidebook navigation and maps** - Guidebooks can be difficult to browse, especially the maps. They work better using the Kindle app on smartphones and tablets.

- **PDFs aren't perfect** - Not all PDFs read well on the Kindle. Text is fine, but images and tables can end up out of place.
- **Cloud collections** - Collections are a way to organise your books. Unfortunately, they aren't easy to manage and can be unreliable when syncing between devices.

Reading Devices: E-reader versus Tablet or Phone

If you read a lot, choose a dedicated e-reader rather than a tablet or smartphone. The e-ink display replicates reading on paper, doesn't tire your eyes, and can be read in bright sunlight. Tablets and smartphones have LCD screens, which are fine for reading for short periods, but will tire your eyes if you read for hours and are difficult to see on the beach. I also prefer having a device that is just for reading, with no distractions.

For occasional reading, a tablet or smartphone that can be used for other tasks makes most sense. They are also better for reading books with visuals or links, such as guidebooks. Simon got rid of his Kindle as he prefers reading on his phone or iPad.

Which E-Book Reader?

I chose an Amazon Kindle Paperwhite, as it's considered the best device, and Amazon has the biggest digital book selection. Their customer service is excellent, and they will readily replace a broken Kindle. I even heard of a traveller who had a new Kindle sent to Thailand at no cost.

Other e-readers are the Barnes & Noble Nook and the Kobo Glo.

Which Kindle?

The Kindle Paperwhite is the best value Kindle. The cheapest model, the Amazon Kindle, doesn't have a light, which is a useful feature for travellers, and the battery life isn't as long. The Kindle Voyage is considerably more expensive and the minor improvements don't seem worth it. The Kindle Fire is a tablet, not a dedicated e-reader.

Each Kindle is available as Wi-Fi only or 3G and Wi-Fi. You pay more upfront for the 3G but don't pay for data usage. I opted for 3G so I can download new books on a beach or train.

Camera

Do You Need One?

Almost every traveller wants a camera to document their trip. As the quality of smartphone cameras has improved, it's easy for everyone to have a camera in their pocket, without adding weight to their luggage.

Which Type of Camera?

Which type of camera to take depends on your interest in photography. A smartphone camera is good enough if all you want are snapshots to share on Facebook and remember your trip by. If you find a smartphone limiting (or aren't travelling with one), take the smallest camera you can get away with.

For camera reviews, see Digital Photography Review and The Wirecutter. Snapsort is a useful site to compare your current camera to a potential new purchase.

Smartphone

If you are happy with the photos your smartphone takes, this is the ideal camera for the carry-on traveller.

Pros

- Fits in your pocket and takes up no space or weight in your luggage
- Never miss a photo opportunity as you will likely have it with you
- Quick and easy to take photos
- Upload photos directly to social media
- Automatically back up photos in the cloud
- More discreet than a large camera
- Easy to edit images using apps

Cons

- Reduced quality in low light

- Too slow for capturing action like sports
- Can't change aperture or shutter speed to achieve different effects
- No variable lens lengths (on most phones) and the digital zoom reduces quality
- Battery life is shorter than most cameras
- No viewfinder and the screen can be difficult to see in bright sunlight

It is certainly possible to use smartphones to take beautiful, creative photos. Casual photographers should consider using one instead of a camera.

Point-and-Shoot Camera

A compact camera offers a step up in quality from a smartphone but can still fit in your pocket.

Pros

- Small and light
- Better quality images than a smartphone
- Often has a long optical zoom
- More discreet than a large camera

Cons

- No interchangeable lenses
- Quality and speed not as good as a mirrorless or DSLR camera
- Not all models have full manual controls

I used to travel with a small Canon PowerShot s95 (the latest model is s120), in addition to my digital SLR, and loved it. It had full manual controls and a wide aperture for low light photos and blurring backgrounds in food photos. The Sony RX100 III also has excellent reviews.

The tiny, robust GoPro is ideal for adventurous activities, as it can be taken anywhere, including into water. The video quality is excellent, and you can capture unique angles with the many available mounts. It's worth considering if you're into video or adventure sports.

DSLR Camera

Digital SLR (single lens reflex) cameras used to be considered the best choice for serious photographers, although mirrorless cameras are becoming more popular, especially with travellers who appreciate their smaller size.

Pros

- High-quality images
- Optical viewfinder
- Full manual controls
- Better battery life than mirrorless cameras
- Huge range of interchangeable lenses

Cons

- Expensive
- Large and heavy

Mirrorless Camera

Mirrorless cameras (also known as Micro Four Thirds) have become popular with serious photographers because they have the features and flexibility of a DSLR but are smaller and lighter.

Pros

- Smaller and lighter than DSLRs
- High-quality images
- Full manual controls
- Interchangeable lenses

Cons

- Expensive
- No optical viewfinder
- Larger and heavier than point and shoot cameras and smartphones

Mirrorless cameras have made heavy SLRs unnecessary for most travellers. They are the perfect compromise between photo quality and weight. If you take photography seriously and feel the limitations of a point and shoot, consider a mirrorless camera.

My Switch From DSLR to Mirrorless

I take photography fairly seriously as I need quality photos to publish on my blog, Never Ending Voyage. I started my travels with a digital SLR with one zoom lens, but despite the minimal kit it still made up a significant amount of weight in my carry-on. I decided to switch to a mirrorless system.

Despite my concern I'd be sacrificing quality, my new camera, an Olympus OM-D EM-5, is better in most ways than my seven-year-old Canon 400D. Mirrorless cameras have come a long way in recent years, and the OM-D EM-5 received rave reviews and convinced many photographers to give up their bulky gear.

I swapped my Canon 400D DSLR and Tamron 18-200mm lens for the Olympus OM-D EM-5 with the 14-42mm kit lens and Panasonic 20mm f1.7 pancake lens. I lost out on the telephoto end, but I decided I wasn't using it enough to justify the weight. I have gained a larger aperture with the 20mm prime lens, which is better for low light and blurring backgrounds.

Olympus OM-D EM-5 Review

Pros

- **Size and weight saving** - Although I had one of the smaller DSLRs, I saved 33% of my previous gear weight (now it's a total of 636 g/1.4 lb), and it takes up less room in my backpack.
- **Higher ISO** - My new setup is much better in low light. I went from a maximum ISO 1600 to up to ISO 25,600 with the Olympus. I have used photos of ISO 6400 on my website.
- **Image stabilisation** - The OM-D EM-5's 5-axis image stabilisation means I can hand-hold the camera at low shutter speeds. Paired with the fast Panasonic 20mm f1.7 lens, which only weighs 100 g (0.22 lb), it's a great low light combo and ideal for food photography.
- **Tilting OLED screen** - I didn't even have a live preview screen on the 400D, so this is a big plus. Being able to tilt it vertically allows for a greater range of shooting angles.

- **Touch screen focusing** - Selecting the area to focus on with one touch is useful.
- **Range of lenses** - It's part of the Panasonic and Olympus Micro Four Thirds system, which offers the biggest range of mirrorless lenses.

Cons

- **Cost** - Mirrorless cameras are more expensive than entry-level DSLRs.
- **Electronic viewfinder** - This takes some adjustment coming from a DSLR, but I quickly got used to it and now switch between the viewfinder and live preview screen.
- **Learning curve** - Coming from an older model Canon, it took a while to learn the many settings and customisable buttons on my Olympus.

My experience with the Olympus OM-D EM-5 has been excellent, and I haven't regretted giving up my DSLR.

There's now a newer model—the Olympus OM-D EM-5 Mark II—which is as well reviewed as its predecessor. Other mirrorless cameras to consider include the Olympus OM-D E-M10 (a cheaper, lighter model), the Sony Alpha a6000, and the Fujifilm X-T1 (expensive but pro-level).

Camera Lenses

The advantage of travelling with a mirrorless or DSLR camera is the range of interchangeable lenses available. Lenses are heavy, so be honest about what you need, and only travel with those you use the most. Unless you have a photography speciality, I recommend sticking to two lenses—a general purpose kit lens (it usually comes bundled with the camera) of around 14-42mm, and a fast 20 or 25mm prime lens. You can't zoom with a prime lens, but they are small, good value, and work well in low light. With this combination, you do miss out on a telephoto, but it's something I rarely use. When I eventually go on safari in Africa, I'll pick up a long zoom for wildlife shots.

Camera Accessories

The same advice applies to camera accessories—keep them to a minimum. How often do you use that flash unit? Will you be bothered to carry around a tripod?

Here are the accessories you are likely to pack:

- **Camera case/bag** - I store my camera and two lenses in a small camera shoulder bag that fits inside my backpack. Some people carry a separate satchel or backpack for their camera gear, but you won't be allowed on all flights with two bags.
- **Storage cards** - The SanDisk Extreme cards are fast and reliable. Pack two or three.
- **Spare batteries** - I have two spare batteries—generic ones are cheaper than the official brand and work fine as spares.
- **Cleaning** - I have a LensPEN cleaning stick and small microfibre cloth.
- **USB cable** - To transfer photos to a laptop (I don't have an SD card slot on my MacBook Air 11-inch).

Electronics Accessories

Cases

For my laptop, iPad, and Kindle I like neoprene cases, like the ones made by Incase, as they are lightweight but offer a decent amount of protection. I have a neoprene sleeve for my iPhone 5 as I store it in my bag. Simon prefers to carry his iPhone 6 naked in his pocket—a risky strategy that I only recommend if you are extremely careful.

International Travel Plug Adapter

You'll need an international power adapter so your device's plug can fit electrical wall outlets around the world. There are 15 types of plugs; each is described by a letter—you can see a full list, images, and map at WorldStandards.eu. The most common are Type A (two square pins used in the US) and Type C (two round pins used in Europe).

I don't need a voltage converter or transformer, as all my devices are multi-voltage—they allow an input of 100–240V, which covers all electrical sockets.

Some older devices, like hair dryers, are single-voltage and only work on one type of power supply, so you'll need a converter to use them abroad—check the input voltage on the plug. It's best to avoid travelling with single-voltage devices.

Power Cables

Simon and I share power cables between devices and with each other to reduce the number we carry. We save space by keeping the Apple laptop power block (the part that plugs into the laptop) but replacing the Apple power cord (the part that plugs into the wall) with a thinner universal power cord (kettle lead). We have one with a Type C European plug and one Type A American style; one of these fits the plugs in almost every country we visit, enabling us to manage with just one international power adapter. I use one of the universal power cords for my camera battery charger, rather than carry a separate cord.

Hard Drive

If you are travelling with a laptop, you need an external hard drive to back up your data. We like the Western Digital My Passport and Seagate Backup Plus Slim hard drives, which are small and light but robust enough for travel. We carry each other's drive so all our data isn't in one place. A case is advisable, but we store ours in a homemade bubble wrap sleeve.

You should expect all hard drives to fail eventually, which is why it's important to have a cloud backup (see the backup section below).

Headphones and Headphone Splitter

Earbuds are the best headphones for travel as they are small. We use Apple EarPods.

We carry a headphone splitter so we can both listen to one iPhone at the same time or watch a film together on the iPad.

HDMI cable

Our HDMI cable is a new addition and not at all essential. We bought it to connect our laptop to TVs so we can watch Netflix or downloaded films on the big screen.

USB Flash Drive

A USB flash drive isn't necessary, but it can be useful for transferring data.

Backing Up

Backing up your data is important for everyone in the digital age, but for travellers it's vital—there's always the chance your laptop is stolen or the hard drive fails due to the rigours of the road. Your data should be backed up in at least two places—we aim for three. Here's the backup system I recommend if you are travelling with a laptop.

Backup 1: External Hard Drive

We travel with a 1 TB hard drive each, which we use to back up everything on our laptops, ideally every day and always before travel days. It's easy to do on a Mac using Time Machine, which is included with the operating system—we just plug the hard drive in and it automatically backs up. When we did need to restore, it was a breeze with Time Machine; it returned everything to the way it was, no need to reinstall any software.

Backup 2: The Cloud

If our bags were stolen, including both laptops and hard drives, we'd be left with nothing. One backup isn't enough for a traveller. Our second backup is online in the cloud. The downside of using a cloud backup is that you need an internet connection. I recommend setting up a cloud service and backing up your data before you leave on your travels, and then backing up whenever you have a connection.

Backblaze

Backblaze automatically backs up everything on your laptop (or you can choose to exclude folders) so it's very easy to use. The initial backup took a long time (over a month on a slow internet connection), but now new files and changes upload quickly. If you ever need to restore, you can download the data or they will FedEx a hard drive to you.

Unlimited data backup with Backblaze costs $5 a month or $50 a year per laptop—well worth it.

Dropbox

We also have a free account with Dropbox, which we use to store some files and sync them across our devices. Dropbox is ideal for backing up important items but not for backing up all your data, as documents need to be stored in the Dropbox folder.

We use it to share files with each other, back up our iPhone photos with the Camera Upload feature, and use apps with Dropbox support to sync content between our phone and laptop.

While I highly recommend a comprehensive cloud backup service like Backblaze, at the very least get a free Dropbox account, and make sure your most important files are backed up there.

Backup 3: Hard Drive With Family

As extra protection, we leave a hard drive with all our files with a relative in the UK and add to it when we return. This isn't an ideal solution, but as we have the above backups, it's extra security so we wouldn't lose absolutely everything. You could also post DVDs or flash drives of data to a family member or friend. We did this with our photos on our first trip.

Photo Backups Without a Laptop

If you are travelling with a camera but don't have a laptop, you still need to back up your photos. Most internet cafes have card readers (or you could travel with one), so you can upload photos to their computers and back up from there—either by transferring them to an external hard drive and/or uploading to an online service like Flickr or Dropbox (but this could be slow, depending on the internet speed). A better option, if you have an iPad, is to use the Camera Connection Kit to transfer your photos to the iPad and from there back up online. If you are serious about photography and are travelling for an extended period, it'll be easier to travel with a laptop.

Smartphone and Tablet Backups

Don't forget to back up the data on your smartphone and tablet too.

For those with Apple devices, you can connect it to your laptop and back up in iTunes, or enable iCloud which backs up your data automatically when you have a Wi-Fi connection. We also have our iPhone photos set to upload to Dropbox.

For Android devices, you can enable backups of accounts, contacts and app configuration in Settings > Accounts, and use Google+ to upload photos. For a full backup, you'll need a backup app.

Go and Back Up!

When travelling with computers, it's not a case of if they're going to fail, but when. Travel subjects these fragile, sensitive devices to abuse—dust, heat, salty air, high humidity, altitude—that they wouldn't encounter in an air-conditioned office. If your data is not in at least two places (preferably miles apart from one another), it doesn't exist.

Having been through the pain of data loss, I can't stress enough the importance of getting a backup plan in place immediately. Don't wait until it's too late. How would you feel if you lost your irreplaceable travel photos? Go and back up now!

Our Electronics List

Laptops and Accessories

- MacBook Pro Retina 15-inch laptop + Incase neoprene case + charger (Simon)
- MacBook Air 11-inch laptop + Incase neoprene case + charger (Erin)
- Western Digital My Passport 1 TB hard drive (Simon)
- Seagate Backup Plus Slim 1 TB hard drive (Erin)
- Small mouse (Simon)
- International travel power adapter
- USB flash drive

- HDMI cable
- Eagle Creek e-Tools Organizer Pro for storing cables and accessories

Photography (Erin)

- Olympus OM-D EM-5 mirrorless camera + Tamrac 3440 Rally Micro shoulder bag
- Olympus 14-42 mm kit lens
- Panasonic 20 mm f1.7 pancake lens
- Charger + 3 batteries
- Sandisk Extreme 16GB SD cards x 2
- USB cable for uploading photos
- Lens pen for cleaning

iPhones, iPad, Kindle, Watch

- iPhone 6 128 GB unlocked + Apple EarPods (Simon)
- iPhone 5 64 GB unlocked + Apple EarPods + Shocksock neoprene sleeve (Erin)
- iPad Pro Wi-Fi 32 GB + neoprene case (Simon)
- Kindle Paperwhite 3G + USB cable + neoprene sleeve (Erin)
- Apple Watch Sport 42mm + USB cable (Simon)
- Apple Pencil for drawing on the iPad Pro
- Plate stand for the iPad
- Apple lightning cables x 2 + USB power adapter
- Headphone splitter

11. Miscellaneous and Luxury Items

Miscellaneous

This section covers everything else you might want to pack. These items are optional and will depend on your trip type. If you are travelling to rural locations in developing countries, you'll need to be more prepared than for a week in Barcelona. Try to keep miscellaneous items to a minimum, and don't get carried away with packing things "just in case."

Travel Towel

Most hotels and guesthouses provide towels, so leave it behind unless you'll be camping or staying in ultra-budget accommodation. Regular towels are bulky and take ages to dry. If you decide to pack one, choose a compact, quick drying travel towel. Simon has a travel towel, which he mostly uses for the beach; I take a sarong instead.

Sarong

Travellers rave about the many uses of a sarong: cover up, skirt, shawl, headscarf, picnic blanket, sheet, window covering. Despite its many uses, I don't recommend a sarong unless you are heading to the beach, and you can buy it there.

Torch (Flashlight)

A torch is useful if you are camping, or visiting places with frequent power cuts (like India and Nepal) or a lack of street lighting. It's also handy for hostel dorm rooms—if you need to catch an early bus, your roommates won't appreciate you turning on the light at 3 a.m.

We don't use a torch often these days, especially as we have one on our iPhone, so we only travel with one between us. I recommend a head torch (headlamp) which keeps your hands free. We have a Petzl Tikka 2, which is light, durable, has a long battery life, three lighting modes (high, low, and flashing), and can be tilted up or down. It's no longer available, but the Petzl Tikkina looks similar.

Duct Tape

Duct tape is a strong, sticky cloth tape that can be torn without scissors. It can fix almost anything: tents, backpacks, shoes, clothes, cables, books, mosquito net holes. Some travellers even use it as blister protection, bandage, sink plug, clothesline, and lint remover. If you are travelling to remote destinations, camping, or hiking, it could be your saviour.

There's no need to pack a large roll. Buy a travel-size roll or create your own by wrapping the tape around a piece of cardboard, plastic card (like an old membership card), pencil, or drinking straw.

Earplugs and Eye Mask

Simon doesn't need these as he can sleep anywhere, but for me, they are essential for a good night's sleep in noisy places and on buses and planes. I use BioEars soft silicone earplugs, which mould to fit your ears, and a cheap eye mask, like the ones given out on planes.

Cable Lock

A cable lock can be used to lock your bag. We've used ours to secure our backpacks under seats on Indian trains and to furniture in budget accommodation. It's not essential but adds a little security, especially if you are staying in very cheap hotels. A retractable cable lock takes up less space.

Sewing Kit

We have a tiny hotel sewing kit with a few needles, buttons, and thread. In many countries, tailors are inexpensive, but this is handy for a quick fix and weighs nothing.

Waterproof and Zip-lock Bags

We use a small, lightweight dry sack for our electronics when doing water sports or going to the beach. An equivalent item is the Sea to Summit Ultra-Sil Nano Dry Sack, which is much lighter than a heavy-duty nylon dry bag. It isn't necessary unless you'll be doing lots of water sports.

I always travel with a few small and medium zip-lock bags for storing food or wet clothes. I prefer the Ziploc brand from the US, as they are durable and close easily.

Toilet Paper

Have some toilet paper on hand for emergencies. There's no need to carry a whole roll—we keep stashes in the small pockets of our backpacks and shoulder bag.

Luxury Items

Travelling with a carry-on doesn't mean you have to give up all luxuries; you just need to minimise them. My luxury items are my camera and third pair of shoes; Simon's are his iPad Pro and AeroPress coffee maker (a new addition that may or may not stay). A friend carries a full-size feather pillow stuffed in a compression bag; others can't live without a hair dryer, straighteners, or high-heel shoes. Artist John Farnsworth (see his interview) travels with a watercolour and oil palette. As long as you are careful with what else you pack, and it all fits in your carry-on, there's no need to deny yourself a luxury or two. You can often find travel-friendly versions that will save you space and weight.

Musical Instruments

Long-term travel is difficult for musicians. Simon was primarily a drummer—not the most practical instrument for travel—but compromised by bringing a Martin Backpacker travel guitar on our first trip around the world and for our first year as digital nomads.

The Martin Backpacker is ideal for travel. It's lightweight and much narrower than a regular guitar but has a full-size neck and surprisingly bright sound. Simon carried it on his shoulder in its soft case along with his backpack. It was a separate piece of luggage, but he usually managed to take both bags on the plane, except on a couple of occasions when he had to check the guitar. (We stuffed the case with clothes and it survived.) Simon no longer travels with it—he wasn't playing enough to justify it—but it is a good option if you are desperate to take an instrument with you.

Other small instruments to consider include a harmonica, mandolin, or ukulele. Just make sure you will use it enough to justify the hassle of carrying it around.

Yoga Mat

If you are serious about yoga, you might want to travel with a yoga mat. Unfortunately, most mats are bulky and heavy, so you need to decide whether it's worth it.

Although there are times when I'd love the convenience of a mat, I've managed without. I attend classes whenever I can, especially in Southeast Asia and Latin America, where classes are inexpensive, and mats are provided. When classes aren't available or are too expensive, I practice with video classes on the Yoga Studio app or from sites like DoYogaWithMe (free), Yogaglo ($18 a month), and Yogaia (€20 a month). I practice on carpet or a rug when available, or on the floor with a towel or blanket to protect my knees. It's not ideal, but it keeps my bag weight down.

If you do want to travel with a yoga mat, choose one that's designed for travel. A popular choice is the Manduka eKo SuperLite Travel Mat, which is foldable for easy storage and made from biodegradable rubber with a grippy surface. It doesn't offer much protection, and although it's one of the lightest mats, it still weighs 907 g (2 lb). Donna Williams highly recommends it and finds it multifunctional: "I have used it to double as a bed, a blanket for extra warmth, a picnic blanket, and even a towel in desperate moments." The Manduka is The Yoga Nomads's top choice in their comparison of five travel yoga mats.

Jenny Krones claims the best travel yoga mat isn't a mat at all. She loves Yoga Paws, which are little yoga mats for your hands and feet. They are small and light and provide excellent grip, although you might need to pair them with a folded towel for knee protection. You can read Jenny's review on Till the Money Runs Out.

Our Miscellaneous Packing List

- Travel towel (Simon)
- Sarong (Erin)
- AeroPress coffee maker (Simon's current experiment. He got rid of the funnel, stirrer, and filter holder to save space.)
- Petzl Tikka 2 head torch (headlamp)
- Small roll of duct tape
- BioEars earplugs (Erin)
- Eye mask (Erin)
- Lifeventure mini retractable cable lock
- Tiny sewing kit
- Pens
- Small dry bag
- Few zip-lock bags
- Toilet paper (a little folded up)
- Moo business cards

12. Documents and Money

Documents

Your most important document is your passport, which should be valid for at least six months after the end of your trip, as it's a requirement of many countries. Make photocopies of your passport and take them with you. We keep two or three in our bags and one in our wallet. Copies make the process easier if you lose your passport and can be used for visa applications. I scan our passports and email them to myself so we always have a digital copy. You could also take a photo of your passport and keep it on your phone for easy access.

Other documents to bring include your driving licence, international driving licence (if needed), vaccination card, yellow fever card (if required by the country you are visiting), scuba diving certification card, and European Health Insurance Card (for EU Citizens travelling in Europe). I store our travel insurance policies on my laptop and keep the policy number and emergency phone number in Simon's wallet.

Money

Debit and Credit Cards

The main way to access your money on the road is by withdrawing cash from ATMs using a debit card. You will find them almost everywhere, and you can withdraw money as you need it, rather than carry vast amounts of cash. Many banks charge high fees for withdrawals abroad, so check your bank's fees and consider changing banks—it could save you a fortune. (See the Best Bank Account section below for more information.)

I recommend taking two debit cards and two credit cards. Bank cards can be stolen, eaten by ATMs, and blocked by your bank, and if you have problems with your card, you won't be able to access your cash. Choose your main bank account from the travel-friendly list below and have a second account as a backup. This could be with your current bank—it doesn't matter as much if it charges high international fees, as you'll only use it if you lose your other card.

Even if you don't plan on using a credit card, it's good to have for emergencies. As my credit cards don't charge international fees, I use them when possible and pay them off in full each month to avoid interest charges. Some travellers use credit cards to accrue frequent flyer points, especially in the US, where there are great deals.

If you are a couple with a joint account, take a card each for the account. If an ATM chews Simon's debit card, we still have access to that account with my card.

An alternative to a debit card is a prepaid card that you load with money in advance and use as a debit card. Our friends recommended it after using one on their round-the-world trip, but these cards don't have the best exchange rates.

Before you leave home, call your bank and tell them when and where you'll be travelling; otherwise, they may block your card due to suspected fraud. Unfortunately, telling them doesn't always help, and they might still block it. In that case, give them a call (I use Skype), and you'll usually get your card unblocked straight away.

Cash

Take some emergency cash. I don't use my cash often, but it's important to have a backup in case you can't find a working ATM. US dollars are the most widely accepted currency, or you could take euros if you are travelling to Europe or nearby countries like Egypt. We travel with a few hundred dollars in a mix of large and small notes. $100 or $50 bills often get better exchange rates; smaller notes are useful for tips and visa fees. Make sure they are in good condition with no tears or marks, as some places can be fussy. Hide a small amount of contingency cash in your luggage in case you lose your main stash.

Traveller's cheques are no longer worth travelling with as they are rarely accepted.

Storing Money and Documents

On travel days, we store our passports, credit and debit cards, and most of our cash in a money belt that we wear under our clothes. Wearing a money belt saved us from losing our valuables when Simon was pickpocketed getting off a crowded bus in Costa Rica. They stole his wallet, but there was only a small amount of cash and one bank card in it; the rest was safe under his clothes. Many people are resistant to wearing a money belt, but I've heard too many stories of travellers having their day bags stolen with their passport and credit cards inside. A bag is too vulnerable for storing your money and documents —always keep them on your person.

Money belts can be hot and uncomfortable, so try to find a thin, lightweight one. A money belt alternative is clothing with hidden pockets—Clever Travel Companion makes underwear, t-shirts, tank tops, and leggings with zippered pockets that are big enough to store a passport. We tried their underwear but found them uncomfortable when sitting down with a passport inside. The tops could work, but for the most security you'd need to wear them under another shirt so that the pocket isn't visible—not ideal in hot climates. Clothing Arts sells pickpocket-proof trousers and shorts with nine or more secure pockets. I've heard good things, but we haven't tried them yet.

Once we arrive at a hotel, we lock our passports and most of our cards and cash inside our backpacks, or in the safe, if available. While we are out, we have a small amount of cash and one card in Simon's wallet. (He carries the money on a day-to-day basis.)

Read the Security chapter for more information about how we keep our possessions safe.

Best Bank Accounts for Travellers

Most banks charge high fees for foreign transactions—accessing your money abroad can cost you a fortune. For example, Lloyds Bank in the UK charges a typical 2.99% foreign exchange fee plus a 1.5% cash withdrawal fee (minimum charge of £2). So withdrawing £200 ($320) costs £8.98 ($14)! You need to find a better option to avoid giving away your hard-earned travel funds to the bank.

Here are some of the best bank accounts for travellers:

United Kingdom

For up-to-date information on the best cards to use abroad, see Money Saving Expert's comprehensive Cheap Travel Money guide.

The current best credit card is the Halifax Clarity Mastercard, which has no foreign exchange or cash withdrawal fees, but as it's a credit card, you pay interest on cash withdrawals. This is the main card we use—I avoid interest by paying off the card as soon as possible after a withdrawal. You could even add money to the account in advance.

The current best debit card is with the Norwich and Peterborough Building Society, which doesn't charge fees for using your card abroad, but you need to pay in at least £500 a month. Metro Bank (London and Southeast England only) doesn't charge fees in Europe, but it does elsewhere.

Our primary travel account is with Nationwide. There are no international fees for spending on the Select credit card, but there are for withdrawing money on the debit card, so we now use our Halifax credit card.

United States

The Charles Schwab High Yield Investor Checking Account is the best option for travellers. It has no foreign usage fees and refunds local fees charged by ATMs worldwide.

The Capital One credit card doesn't charge foreign transaction fees.

Australia

The 28 Degrees Mastercard credit card doesn't charge international fees for purchases, but it does to withdraw cash.

Please note that bank terms and conditions often change, and the information above may go out of date. It is important to research the best bank account before making your final choice.

Our Documents and Money List

- Passport
- Dollars
- 2 debit and 3 credit cards each
- Card reader for online banking (issued by our bank for secure access)
- Driving licence
- International driving licence (when needed)
- Photocopies of passport
- Passport photos (for visa applications)
- Vaccination card
- Yellow fever vaccination card
- Scuba diving certification card
- European Health Insurance Card (when in Europe)
- Money belt
- Wallet (Simon) including a copy of our passports and travel insurance details

13. What Not to Pack

Learning what *not* to pack is essential for packing light. You need to discover what you can leave behind—the items that seem like they might come in handy but, in all honesty, you can do without.

Restricted Items

If you are flying, make sure everything you pack is allowed on the plane in your carry-on. See Airline Restrictions for more information about the things you can't take, including penknives and large bottles of toiletries.

Unnecessary Items

When planning your trip, it's easy to get carried away when reading packing lists and browsing outdoor stores. They entice you with all sorts of fancy gear, and you start to panic that maybe you need those things too. Resist the urge to add those "might be useful" items to your bag—you don't need them.

Here are common items on packing lists that as a carry-on traveller you should *not* pack. The exception is if you've decided that something is so important that you are going to take it as your luxury item. As long as it fits in your carry-on, you could pack one or two inessential things.

- **Towel** - They are bulky, heavy, and take ages to dry. Most accommodation provides one, so there's no need to lug one around. You may need a towel in ultra-budget hotels or for the beach, but in that case, take a lightweight travel towel or sarong instead.

- **Heavy Jacket** - Only take a jacket if your entire trip is in cold places and you can wear it on travel days. Otherwise, use layers to keep warm, and buy a coat if necessary when you reach the cold. The exception is an ultralight down jacket, which packs down small (see the Cold Weather chapter for details).
- **Hiking boots** - Most people don't need them. If you'll be trekking, hiking shoes or trail runners are smaller and more versatile—we hiked for five days in the Nepal Himalayas wearing them. You can often rent boots in major trekking destinations if needed.
- **Tent** - It takes up a lot of space and is only worth it if you'll be camping most of the time (in which case look for an ultralight tent). You can rent camping gear if you need it for a trek.
- **Sleeping bag** - As with a tent, you need to use this all the time to make it worthwhile. We rented one locally for hiking in the Himalayas and the Salt Flats jeep tour in Bolivia.
- **Sleep sheet/sleeping bag liner** - I've never needed one as I avoid accommodation with questionable sheets. If you are an ultra budget traveller or germaphobe, *maybe* consider a lightweight silk version.
- **Mosquito net** - Most hotels provide one when needed.
- **Hammock** - I love hammocks, but they are too heavy to carry around.
- **Hair dryer and straighteners** - In hot weather your hair dries quickly, and many hotels provide dryers.
- **Expensive jewellery** - You'll be a target for thieves.
- **High-heel shoes**- For nights out, pack attractive sandals or ballet flats instead. They are more versatile, comfortable, and take up less space.
- **Washing line** - You can always find somewhere to hang your clothes.
- **Sink plug** - If there's no plug, I find a sock works well enough for doing laundry.
- **Laundry detergent** - Use shampoo or soap instead, or buy small packets locally.
- **Travel pillow** - I've never needed one. Try using a folded sweater instead.
- **Plates, bowls, and cups** - Hostel kitchens and apartment rentals provide these, or you can improvise.
- **Umbrella** - Buy one when you arrive if you need to; I rarely do.

- **Power voltage transformer** - This is built into most electronics.
- **Power strip** - Some digital nomads pack one to charge multiple devices at once. We can always find enough power sockets for our laptops and charge our smaller devices via USB.
- **Guidebooks** - They are bulky and heavy. Use a guidebook for planning before you leave and rip out the sections you need. Or better yet, buy an e-book for your smartphone, tablet, or e-reader.

PART THREE

Preparing for Departure

14. How to Pack

Packing Organisers

When you are travelling with a carry-on, *how* you pack is just as important as *what* you pack. The best way to stay organised and save space is to use packing organisers—many carry-on travellers swear by them. They could be simple zip-lock bags or more durable packing cubes or compression bags. By using organisers, you can compartmentalise your gear with each bag or cube containing a different category of item.

Using packing organisers has many advantages:

- **Pack more efficiently** - It's easy to pack when you know what goes in each cube and how each cube fits in your luggage. It's like a game of Tetris—rearrange the cubes and other items until they fit perfectly into your bag, and then stick with your system. You'll feel less stressed when packing, as you know everything will fit.
- **Find things easily** - Your cubes work like drawers at home. You know what's in them, so you can take out the relevant cube rather than rummaging around at the bottom of your suitcase.
- **Save space** - You can squeeze a surprising amount of clothes into a cube, so you can pack more. Compression bags are even better as they remove excess air.
- **Keep clothes clean and dry** - Some organisers are water resistant and

all offer protection from dirt. They can also be used to protect clothes in dusty hotel drawers.

- **Prevent overpacking** - Limit what you pack by choosing an organiser for each category. I know that one large cube is enough for all my clothes. If I buy a new item and it fits in the cube, I can take it with me; if not, something else has to go.

Creating your own packing system will make carry-on travel much easier—I highly recommend trying it. There are a number of options:

Compression Bags

If you are struggling to fit everything into your carry-on, consider compression bags. These are sealable plastic bags with one-way pressure valves that let air out but not in. By removing excess air, your clothes are compressed, and you save space. They work particularly well for bulkier items like fleeces and sweaters, so they are useful for cold climates.

As the bags are airtight, they keep your clothes clean and dry—good to know if you get caught in a heavy rain shower or on a small boat with sea spray.

Compression bags are simple to use. You fold your clothes and lay them flat inside the bag, seal the zip-lock top, then roll the bag, squeezing out all the air. It helps to do this on the floor and perhaps kneel on it to use your body weight to squeeze out as much air as possible.

When choosing a compression bag, make sure it is suitable for travel—you should be able to remove the air by rolling it rather than with a vacuum cleaner. Some compression bags are flimsy and tear easily; it's worth investing in a durable bag, as it's difficult to find replacements abroad. Compression bags come in a range of sizes. You can choose a large bag for all your clothes or smaller bags to separate items.

The downsides of compression bags are that your clothes get a little creased; you have to uncompress the bag to access items—not very convenient if you need something on a travel day—and they can tear, which is why it's worth paying more for a sturdy bag. It can also take effort to roll the bag, especially if it's full. I admit I got Simon to roll mine whenever possible, as he was better at removing the air than I was.

I've tried a range of compression bags. My favourite is the robust Packmate travel roll storage bag (UK only) which comes with a five-year guarantee and free replacements of the slider that seals the bag. The Eagle Creek Pack-it compression sac is also excellent—the plastic is nylon reinforced, and it is covered by Eagle Creek's lifetime warranty.

Don't confuse plastic rollable compression bags with compression sacks made from nylon, like those used to store a sleeping bag. Some travellers use these, but you are better off with compression bags, which remove more air, or packing cubes, which keep your clothes more organised and accessible.

For five years we both travelled with a large compression bag for our clothes. They worked well, but we eventually tired of rolling the bags and switched to a new type of compression packing cube.

Packing Cubes

Packing cubes are zippered fabric containers, usually in a rectangular shape, for organising your items and making them easier to find in your luggage. They come in a range of sizes and are often sold as sets. Unlike compression bags, you can use them to organise all kinds of gear, not just clothes. For example, you could have one large cube for your clothes, a small cube for underwear, and another for your electronic accessories—chargers, cables, etc. You know exactly where each item is kept, and when you need it, you just take out the appropriate cube.

Packing cubes have some advantages over compression bags: it's easier to access your clothes, as you don't need to release the air; they are more durable; they stack neatly in your luggage; and your clothes will be less creased. The downside is that, although they take up less room compared to packing your clothes loose, they don't compress as much as a bag designed for that purpose.

Popular packing cube brands include Eagle Creek, eBags, REI, and Sea to Summit. If you have a Tortuga Backpack, you can buy a set of three Tortuga packing cubes that fit perfectly inside. Tom Bihn also sells custom cubes for their bags.

When choosing packing cubes, durability is the most important attribute—you want a strong material with quality zips so that you can stuff as much in as possible without them breaking. The size and other features come down to personal preference and how you want to organise your things. Many cubes have a mesh top for breathability and so you can see inside—I don't find this necessary as I know what's in my three cubes. If you buy cubes in different sizes and colours, identification is easy. This is useful for families sharing a suitcase—each family member could have a different coloured cube.

Eagle Creek Packing Cubes Review

I'm a big fan of Eagle Creek's packing cubes. The build quality is excellent, and they come with a lifetime warranty. I have used a half (small size) Eagle Creek Pack-It packing cube with a mesh top for six years of constant travel, and it's still going strong.

When we decided to switch from compression bags to packing cubes, we tried Eagle Creek compression cubes, which are like ordinary cubes but with a compression zipper around the side that squeezes them into a smaller size. They turned out to be the perfect compromise. We could fit everything we needed into the cube, but it's easier to use than a compression bag, with quick access and no need for rolling.

Simon uses the Eagle Creek Pack-It compression cube with a mesh top—he uses one full (large size) cube for all his clothes and underwear. The advantage of the classic design is that it has more structure and unzips on three sides for easy access.

I use the Eagle Creek Pack-It Specter compression cubes—a full cube for my main clothes and a half cube for my workout clothes. The Specter cubes are the lightest on the market, made from ultra lightweight, translucent silnylon ripstop. They are more expensive than the mesh cubes but are water and stain resistant, and are amazingly light. A full Specter cube weighs just 28 g (1 oz) compared to 113 g (4 oz) for the mesh cube. The Specter compression cubes are heavier (57 g/2 oz) but still much lighter than the mesh compression cube (134 g/4.7 oz). The downside of the Specter cubes is that they only unzip part the way around, not on three sides like most cubes. This makes clothes slightly less accessible, but as I roll my clothes, I can reach in and grab what I need.

Packing Cubes or Compression Bags?

Packing cubes are easier to use than compression bags, so I recommend starting with them. If you are struggling to fit everything in or are travelling in cold weather, try a compression bag instead. A compression bag could also be used to bring home clothes purchased on your trip. Even if you use a compression bag for your clothes, packing cubes are useful for organising other items.

Electronic Accessories Organisers

If you travel with as many electronics as we do, you will have lots of accessories that need organising—cables, chargers, hard drives, etc. Any packing cube would work to store these things, but mesh tops aren't ideal; a water resistant material with more protection is preferable.

We used to have a clear plastic packing cube to store our electronics accessories, plus miscellaneous gear like head torches, sewing kit, and cable lock. Everything was loose, so it became messy and difficult to find what we needed. We now use the Eagle Creek eTools Organizer Pro, which has lots of internal pockets and cable loops, so our gear is much more organised. It's a little heavier than a standard cube, but the case is durable and water resistant. I think it's worth it for the protection and organisation.

Toiletry Bags

You don't need a fancy toiletry bag, but choose something small and light. We use the Lifeventure Ultralite Wash Holdall, which is lightweight and has a pocket for small items, a built-in mirror, and a hook to hang it up when there's nowhere to put it. The Sea to Summit Travelling Light Hanging Toiletry Bag is a similar lightweight case.

Shoe Bags

Some travel companies sell bags especially for storing shoes in your luggage. These could be handy, but I've never found them necessary. If I haven't had a chance to clean my shoes before packing them, I use a regular plastic bag to keep my backpack clean. You can even use a shower cap to store your shoes.

My Tieks ballet flats come with a storage pouch.

Ultimately, it doesn't matter which bags or cubes you decide on—you could even use simple zip-lock bags—but make sure you do have an organisational system. It'll create more space in your luggage and make packing and finding items so much easier.

Create a Packing List

Before you start packing, write a list of everything you plan to take. It will help you stay organised, prevent fears that you've forgotten something, and stop you from panic-packing at the last minute.

After a test pack, you might need to refine the original list, reducing or changing items as needed so that everything fits comfortably in your carry-on. When you do your final pack, print the list (or use an app) and tick off items as you pack them. Stick strictly to the list and don't add things "just in case."

A packing list will also help you pack for your next trip if you note anything you didn't use or often wear, so you can learn what you truly need.

I have created a customisable packing list, which you can download at carryontravels.com.

Test Pack

Don't leave packing until the day before you leave—do a test pack in advance. If you are going on a long trip, you might do this a couple of weeks before you leave; otherwise, allow at least a few days.

Lay out everything on your packing list and ask yourself what you'll be using it for. If it's for a "what if" scenario or for an event far in advance (like snorkelling gear for Thailand in five months), leave it behind. Reduce as much as you can and then pack everything. Go for a 15 to 30-minute walk wearing your backpack or rolling your suitcase and see how it feels. This might convince you to get rid of even more things. When you've reduced as much as you can and everything fits comfortably in your carry-on, update your packing list to use as a checklist for your final pack.

How to Pack

Roll or fold: If you are using a compression bag, lay your clothes flat inside it before you roll. For packing cubes (or loose clothes), fold your clothes lengthwise and then roll them as tightly as possible—this will take up less space than folded clothes and minimise wrinkles.

Use every space: You have limited space in a carry-on, so be creative—stuff socks or other items in shoes, and use all available pockets of space. I usually find I can squeeze small things in the bottom corners of my backpack.

Liquids: Even if you're not flying, store your liquids in a zip-lock bag within your toiletries bag in case of leakage.

Accessible pockets: Keep anything you'll need during the journey accessible. I keep my earplugs, eye mask, tissue, and travel sickness pills in the front pocket of my backpack where I can reach them on long journeys. If I know I'll need my fleece, I strap it to the outside of my backpack using the compression straps.

Weight distribution: If you are travelling with a backpack, you want the weight to be centred and close to your body to minimise the pull on your shoulders. To do this, pack your heaviest items, such as shoes or camera, towards the centre of the bag close to your back and lighter items below and above them. Honestly, I don't worry too much about this, as it's less of a concern with carry-on backpacks than with large, heavy hiking backpacks.

Develop your system: Packing cubes make it straightforward to pack your bag, and you'll soon discover the best way to organise things. Experiment with a few methods of fitting everything in, and once you have a system, stick to it. This will make it quicker to pack, and you'll notice if anything is missing.

15. Overcoming Concerns

Wearing Clothes More than Once

I usually wear my clothes more than once before I wash them (except underwear and socks), and if you are travelling with a limited wardrobe, you probably will too. This might seem unhygienic if you are used to automatically throwing your clothes into the laundry basket at the end of the day, but you'll discover that clothes don't need to be washed as much as you think. I am so used to this now that even when I have access to a washing machine, I don't wash after one wear as it feels wasteful (of water, detergent, electricity, time) and will wear my clothes out more quickly.

This doesn't mean I wear clothes that are smelly or dirty. There are ways you can help your clothes stay fresh with multiple wears:

- Shower every day and use deodorant. (I like the natural Salt of the Earth crystal stick.)
- Hang up your clothes after wearing to air them out.
- Do a sniff test to decide if it's good to wear another time.
- If you get a small stain on your clothes, wash that area with soap and water in the sink rather than washing the whole item.
- For exercise clothes (or if you'll be very active), choose technical fabrics with antimicrobial properties to repel sweat. I love Athleta's Unstinkable fabric. Merino wool is another odour resistant fabric

used by brands like Icebreaker and SmartWool—ultra light travellers who travel with just two t-shirts swear by it.

Other travellers have suggested taking a travel-size bottle of Febreze to spray your clothes with, packing fabric softener sheets in with your clothes, and using a tiny amount of essential oil on the armpits of clothes.

How often I wash my clothes depends on what I've been doing. If I've been sweating heavily on a hike or a day out sightseeing in the tropics, I'll wash tops after one wear; if I've been sitting at my laptop in an air conditioned room, it won't be necessary. Trousers, skirts, and shorts can be worn more frequently than tops.

If the idea of wearing clothes more than once still grosses you out, there's no reason you can't fit seven tops into your carry-on and do laundry once a week.

Laundry

Yes, travelling with fewer clothes means you have to do laundry more often. With the recommended packing list in this book, you'll need to do laundry about once a week, but it doesn't have to be difficult, and there are a number of options.

Laundry Service

In many places laundry services are common and affordable. In Southeast Asia and Latin America, you'll pay around $1 per kilo (2.2 lb) of laundry for someone to wash and dry your clothes and return them to you neatly folded the same or following day. A complete load of laundry for both of us costs $2-4 and is well worth it.

In general, avoid hotel laundry services that charge per item, as this can be expensive.

Self Service Laundrette

In more developed countries in Europe, the US, or Australia, you'll have to do your own laundry if you're on a budget. You can find coin-operated washing machines in hostels, motels, or laundrettes (laundromats).

Rent Apartments with Washing Machines

I often rent apartments, using sites like Airbnb, and sometimes have access to a washing machine, which makes life easier. You can even choose a washing machine as one of the amenities you require when doing a search.

Hand-Wash

Sometimes I hand-wash my clothes in hotel sinks—usually just a few pairs of underwear or a t-shirt to tide me over until a big wash. It's not necessary to carry laundry detergent; I occasionally buy small packets locally but mostly use shampoo or shower gel (especially if the hotel provides it), which foams well, or soap, if there's nothing else. If there's no sink plug, a sock works well enough.

Some travellers pack a large, heavy-duty zip-lock bag called an Aloksak, which is completely waterproof and has been approved by the US Navy. You can use this as a makeshift washing machine by adding your dirty clothes, laundry detergent, and hot water, and mixing everything by hand. Then seal the bag and allow the clothes to soak in the soapy water for 10 minutes or so before rinsing in clean water. I've never tried this method, but if you'll be doing a lot of hand-washing (perhaps if you are on a budget in countries without cheap laundry services), it's worth considering.

Drying your clothes can be an issue when you are hand-washing. It'll be quicker to dry them outside if you can—perhaps on your balcony, or the hotel might have a washing line in the garden or on the roof. On a sunny day, they will only take a few hours to dry. Otherwise, hang your clothes up in your room on any available surface—shower rail, clothes hangers, backs of chairs, radiators, etc. It's best to keep them in the bathroom while they are still dripping to avoid damaging any furniture or floor boards. You can speed up the drying time by wringing clothes well, laying each item on a travel towel, and rolling it up to squeeze out excess moisture. If you'll be hand-washing your clothes often, choosing quick drying clothes is especially important.

Storing Your Dirty Laundry

It's best to do most of your laundry before travel days so that you don't have to store it separately from your clean clothes. I use a large zip-lock bag for dirty laundry. Simon stuffs his in the front compartment of his backpack. Many backpacks have pockets and mesh compartments that can be used for this. Some packing cubes, like the Eagle Creek Pack-It Clean Dirty Cube, are designed for this purpose with two compartments—one for clean and one for dirty clothes.

It may seem daunting if you're not used to being without a washing machine, but laundry is a problem that every traveller has, and in popular destinations there are many services to help you.

Wearing the Same Clothes

You might worry that you'll be bored of wearing the same clothes or feel self-conscious that you're always seen in the same outfit. It doesn't take long to get used to a limited wardrobe, and it becomes a blessing not to waste time deciding what to wear. If you've made sure all your clothes go together, you can mix and match to create different outfits or liven them up with accessories like jewellery from your travels—it'll make a portable memento too.

If you get sick of the same outfits, you can replace them as you travel. Buying clothes locally is often inexpensive, and they'll be suitable to the climate. In places like India and Vietnam, you can even get clothes tailor-made at low costs.

If you're staying in one place for a longer period, you could buy a few extra items for while you are there. I rarely do this, as I've become so used to a small wardrobe that it doesn't feel necessary.

You'll discover that people don't care what you wear, or even notice. Do you remember what your friends wore the last three times you saw them?

When you travel, you move outside your comfort zone, normal routine, and social circles. Changing your attitude to clothes is part of this. When you're exploring the world and seeing new and exciting things every day, your outfit is no longer as important, and it's not something you want to spend your time worrying about.

Being Unprepared

One of the most common concerns is being unprepared for different situations. What if it rains? Or turns cold? Or you get invited to a fancy party?

If you've followed the advice in this book and packed smart, you should have what you need for a wide variety of circumstances. For everything else, remember you can buy it there.

Mike Sowden of Fevered Mutterings recently travelled for the first time with just a carry-on. He described his epiphany:

"I've now found (through watching you guys and other experienced travellers) that amazingly, other places have stuff too. So there's no need to take 50% of the clutter I panic-pack because I assume that I can't get it elsewhere. Most of the time? Elsewhere has it covered. I think that's the key to carry-on travel."

Souvenirs and Gifts

You might want to buy souvenirs or gifts for friends and family. First, ask yourself: Do you truly need it? Are you going to use it back home or will it just add clutter to your life?

Consider buying small and lightweight souvenirs, especially wearable items like jewellery or scarves that can liven up your carry-on wardrobe.

If there is something you really want to buy and you can't fit it in your carry-on, you could send a parcel home. On our first trip we sent back parcels from India, Nepal, Indonesia, and Australia. (We even posted a didgeridoo, which we never used!) Post offices sell boxes and packing supplies, and they usually have English speakers who can explain the postage options. As we were on a long trip and in no hurry, we chose sea mail, which is the cheapest and slowest method. It took a few months, but everything made it home.

If you have a lot of shopping to do, you could save it until the end of your trip and buy a cheap bag to check in on your way home. Or if your airline allows two bags, fill up a small backpack with souvenirs as your personal item.

Airline Restricted Items

Don't let airline restrictions stop you from travelling light. Are those items worth the hassle of checking in your luggage?

Remember that things like penknives, large scissors, and toiletries over 100 ml (3.4 oz) are only restricted on the plane. Once you reach your destination, you can buy them if needed—it will cost less than checking your luggage would have.

If you are concerned about travelling without an item like a penknife, try it once and you might be surprised by how little you miss it.

It's Just Not Possible

If, despite all the advice in this book, travelling with a carry-on still seems impossible to you, then see it as a gradual process. For your next holiday, pack as usual and write a list of everything you take. During your trip mark how often you use each item. It might astonish you how much you packed you didn't need. For subsequent trips, you'll have proof of what you really need and can pack less each time.

For inspiration, check out the interviews in Part 4 and the list of other carry-on travellers in Appendix B. If they can do it, so can you.

16. Security and Travel Insurance

Keeping Your Gear Safe

When you are travelling the world, you are vulnerable to theft, especially on travel days when you have all your belongings with you and may be tired from a long journey. Security is something we're always aware of—we aim to be careful but not paranoid. We've been lucky that the only thing we've had stolen was a wallet containing $20 and a debit card when Simon was pickpocketed.

Travelling with a carry-on gives you a security advantage, as you'll always have your bag with you on buses and planes, but you still need to be careful. Here are some tips for keeping your belongings safe:

Lock your luggage - Choose a suitcase or front-opening backpack that is lockable with a small combination lock, and make sure it's locked on travel days to prevent anyone grabbing something inside.

Wear a money belt - On travel days, wear a money belt under your clothes (or clothes with a hidden pocket) containing your passport, cards, and most of your cash. If you keep your valuables in your bag, it's too easy for it to be stolen, and you'll lose everything. Simon was wearing a money belt when he was robbed and would have lost a lot more than $20 if he hadn't been.

Leave your valuables in the hotel - Once you reach your destination, leave your valuables (passports, cash, cards, electronics) in the hotel safe in your room or locked inside your luggage. When we feel it's necessary, we attach our backpacks to a solid piece of furniture using a light cable lock. This may not prevent a determined thief, but it does stop opportunistic theft. Leaving your valuables out on display is an unnecessary risk.

Carry a small amount of cash - When you are out exploring, only carry a small amount of cash and one credit or debit card in your wallet. Leave your backup cards and spare cash at the hotel. I also recommend leaving your driving licence behind unless you'll be driving, as it'll be difficult to replace if it gets stolen. We keep a copy of our passports in our wallet in case we need ID.

Keep your luggage close - Don't store your luggage in overhead compartments on buses or trains, as it could be stolen without you noticing. It's best to keep it under your seat or by your feet, but stay aware because it could be stolen from the seat behind you or slashed and the contents removed.

Use zippered pockets - If possible, wear trousers and shorts with hidden zippered pockets for carrying your wallet and phone. Simon's iPod Touch was in his zippered pocket when he was robbed, and the thieves didn't get it. If he had two zippered pockets, it might have saved his wallet too.

Be careful in crowded places - Be especially aware of your valuables in crowded places like markets and train stations. When we're surrounded by a dense crowd, Simon keeps his hands in his pockets, and we make sure our shoulder bag and camera are in front of us. It helps to wear a bag with a strap that crosses your body. Don't rush to get off a crowded bus—wait for everyone else to leave first.

Be aware of scams - Scams are used to distract your attention in order to steal your wallet or bag. For example, someone sprays you with ketchup or another substance and then tries to clean it off, or drops something on the floor and waits for you to help. The "Dangers and Annoyances" section in Lonely Planet guidebooks is worth a read before you arrive, or google "scams" and the name of your destination, especially if it's a big city.

Keep your bag close in cafés - In public places like cafés, wrap your bag's strap around your legs to prevent anyone grabbing it, and don't leave your phone or wallet on the table. If you take your laptop to a café, choose a corner table furthest from the door.

Trust your instincts - Be aware of your surroundings—if something doesn't feel right, get yourself out of the situation.

Stay sober - Avoid getting drunk as you'll be especially vulnerable, or at least don't take valuables out when you'll be drinking.

Take a taxi at night - This isn't necessary everywhere, but it's a good idea in big cities, particularly if you've been drinking. Ask locals for advice if you're not sure if it's safe to walk.

Hopefully these tips will keep you safe, but if the worst happens and you are robbed, first call your bank and cancel any stolen cards. You'll need a police report to claim on your insurance for lost items. For a temporary replacement passport, contact your embassy or consulate—it helps to have copies of your passport.

Travel Insurance

Travel insurance is a must. If you have a medical emergency and need to be flown to your home country, it could cost thousands of dollars. Here's what to look for in a travel insurance policy:

- Read the small print before buying a policy, or you'll waste your money if they don't pay out.
- Medical is the most important type of coverage—make sure it includes emergency evacuation and repatriation.
- Check which activities the policy includes. You often pay extra for high-risk activities such as scuba diving, white water rafting, high-altitude trekking, and horse riding.
- Most policies charge extra for skiing and snowboarding. You might just want to purchase a winter sports policy for the time you are in the mountains.
- It's unlikely the standard policy will cover valuables like cameras and laptops (or the limit will be low), so you may need to pay extra (see

the electronics section below).

- Other types of coverage to look for are baggage and cancellation. To save money, we have a basic policy without these, but include them if you can.
- Choose a worldwide policy if you don't know where you'll be travelling. Otherwise, it's cheaper to exclude the US or focus on one region.
- Check the excess/deductible (the contribution you'll pay towards a claim). The higher the excess, the cheaper the policy, but make sure you can afford it if anything goes wrong.
- If you are travelling with a one-way ticket with no definite plans to return home, check that you aren't required to have a return ticket.
- If your trip is for less than a month and you travel a few times a year, look into annual multi-trip travel insurance policies, which can work out cheaper than a policy for each trip.

Renewing Travel Insurance While Travelling

We started with a one-year backpacker insurance policy like many round-the-world travellers, but unlike them, after a year we carried on travelling. We discovered we couldn't extend our policy, and other policies we looked at required us to be living in the UK at the time of purchase.

If you need to renew your policy while abroad, make sure your insurance company allows this—my recommended travel insurance policies below do.

How to Find Travel Insurance

You can use insurance comparison websites like MoneySupermarket.com (UK) and SquareMouth.com (USA/Canada) to compare the price and coverage of different policies. For trips of a year or more where you might need to renew, or if you don't have a return ticket, I recommend one of the policies below.

True Traveller Insurance (UK and Europe)

We have used True Traveller for four years now, and it's the best value policy I've found for long-term travellers from the UK and Europe. They were originally an adventure travel company, not an insurance broker, so they understand the needs of long-term travellers. On their user-friendly website you can tailor the policy to suit you, choosing basic medical insurance or adding extras like baggage, electronics, cancellation, activities, and winter sports coverage. Most importantly, True Traveller allows you to buy a policy when you are already travelling and don't have a return ticket, so it's ideal for digital nomads and long-term travellers. You can also extend your insurance and receive a 10% discount on the regular price.

You can get a quote from **TrueTraveller.com**.

World Nomads (Worldwide)

World Nomads are a well-respected travel insurance company, which we used on our round-the-world trip. They allow you to buy a policy when you are already travelling and are popular with many long-term travellers. They cover most nationalities, so if you aren't from the UK or Europe, this is the policy I recommend.

We no longer use them because they are more expensive than True Traveller —our policy costs over double the price. The World Nomads policy is more comprehensive and includes baggage and cancellation, but these aren't things we need.

You can get a quote from **WorldNomads.com**.

Electronics Insurance

Most travel insurance policies do not cover electronics like laptops, cameras, tablets, and smartphones, or the coverage limit is very low. You may be able to pay extra to insure your electronics, or check if they are covered under your home insurance policy.

We have a separate policy with Photoguard (UK only), which covers our camera and laptops for accidental damage and theft. You can get a quote from Photoguard.co.uk. Clements in the US covers electronics for long-term travellers.

If you choose not to insure your electronics—we don't insure our iPhones or iPad—make sure you have a fund to cover their replacement if they are stolen.

Whatever you decide, do buy medical travel insurance. If the worst happens, you'll want to be covered, or it could cost you more than you can afford.

PART FOUR

Interviews with Carry-On Travellers

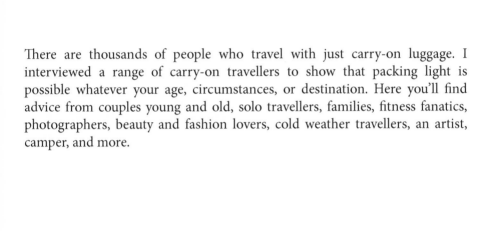

There are thousands of people who travel with just carry-on luggage. I interviewed a range of carry-on travellers to show that packing light is possible whatever your age, circumstances, or destination. Here you'll find advice from couples young and old, solo travellers, families, fitness fanatics, photographers, beauty and fashion lovers, cold weather travellers, an artist, camper, and more.

17. Brandon Quittem and Anne Rapp - The Yoga Nomads

Brandon and Anne are travelling yoga teachers who love street food, beaches, trekking, and staying healthy on the road.

1) Where have you travelled with just a carry-on?

We've been travelling for 18 months with only carry-on backpacks. Countries include India, Sri Lanka, Nepal, Thailand, Vietnam, Cambodia, Myanmar, Philippines, Indonesia, Singapore, Japan, Costa Rica, and Nicaragua.

2) What are the advantages and disadvantages of travelling with a carry-on? Do you think it's worth it?

First off, the advantages by far outweigh the disadvantages.

Advantages:

- Save money on flights because we never pay to check bags. (We saved $500+ in 2014.)
- Increased mobility - With compact packs, travel days are a breeze. And when looking for accommodation, we can comfortably walk for

miles without any issues.

- Voluntary simplification of our lives - We soon realised how little we really needed—a powerful realisation that impacted our future in a profound way.

Disadvantages:

- We can only pack for one or two climates at a time. This works well for us since we like travelling in warm countries. However, we did spend a month trekking in Nepal in freezing temperatures, and we made it work just fine.

3) What luggage do you use and what do you like or not like about it?

Anne: Osprey Farpoint 40L (S/M) – Fantastic pack that's super comfy, very durable, and well organised, but it could use hip pads.

Brandon: Tortuga V2 – I absolutely love this pack. It fits a surprising amount and has nice hip pads and a laptop compartment. It could use more internal structure so the weight is better supported on your hips.

4) Do you travel with a day bag in addition to your main carry-on?

Yes. Anne uses a collapsible REI Flashpack 22L, which is decent; however, she would like more organisation pockets. I use the Datsusara Battlepack Mini, which is a new obsession. It feels great, is made out of hemp, is super durable and well organised, and has a cool design.

5) How do you manage the limited carry-on weight allowance many airlines have? Have you ever been forced to check-in your bag?

We have never had any real issues with weight allowances. One time we were over the allowed weight, and we just moved a couple of heavier items from our carry-on pack into our daypacks, and we were in the clear. 90% of the time, the airlines don't even weigh our "small carry-on backpacks."

6) Tell us about how you've managed to camp and do multi-day hikes with just a carry-on.

Packing smart is all it takes to convert your carry-on backpack into a camping machine. Be sure to use ultra light gear and pack technical clothes. Both will cut down weight and bulk.

7) What clothes and shoes do you travel with? Are there any particular brands or fabrics that you recommend?

Anne: New Balance Minimus trainers and flip-flops are all she needs! Anne also loves Lululemon's technical clothing.

Brandon: Chacos and flip-flops are all I travel with. Chacos are the best travel shoes in the world. They have great arch support and are very sturdy to support your feet when you've got a big pack on. I've used them for gruelling three-day volcano hikes in Indonesia, exploring the underbelly of Mumbai, and everywhere in between.

8) What technology do you pack?

As a couple we travel with:

- 2 MacBook Airs (one 13-inch and one 11-inch)
- Olympus EM-5 mirrorless camera + 2 lenses
- 2 Kindles
- iPhone 5
- Samsung Galaxy S4
- GoPro Hero 4
- Western Digital external hard drive (2 TB)
- All the required cords. (We only use one cord for both Kindles and Samsung Galaxy S4.)

9) As yoga teachers, do you carry yoga gear with you?

Yes, we travel with one Manduka eKO Superlite Travel Mat. It only weighs 907 g (2 lb) and can be folded or rolled. It works great rolled up and attached vertically to the side of the Tortuga. We also have one Manduka microfibre towel, which is multipurpose: beach towel, shower towel, yoga towel, and even my blanket.

10) Did you pack anything that you regretted or got rid of?

Anne originally brought a hair dryer but never used it. She ditched it after a month.

11) How do you organise your things in your luggage?

We highly recommend stuff sacks or compression sacks to organise and compress your clothes and gear. I use four different compression sacks in my Tortuga. One for shirts, pants, underwear/socks, and electronics. Then I usually have a plastic bag for dirty clothes. This allows me to be super organised and pack more into the space I have. It also makes finding an item of clothing super easy.

12) Do you have any other tips for packing light?

Focus on minimising your bulky items: shoes, sweatshirts, jackets, long pants, etc. You really don't need tons of layers if you're travelling near the equator.

Bring versatile items only. For example, I have one pair of pants, PrAna Bronsons, and they are used for trekking, staying warm, or dressing up for a restaurant/bar. This takes the place of trekking pants, sweatpants, and jeans.

Try to minimise cords for your electronics. We use one micro SD cord to charge one phone and two Kindles.

We always bring a foot rubz ball when travelling. It's just a smaller rubber ball used to loosen the fascia on the bottom of your feet. It helps keep my body in line after long travel days, trekking, or just exploring a city. I massage my feet with it every day no matter what.

You can see Anne and Brandon's packing list and follow their travels on their blog, The Yoga Nomads.

18. Lori and Randy Grant - The Retirees

When faced with an empty nest after their son left for college, Lori and Randy decided to sell everything that wouldn't fit into their carry-on bags, retire early from their teaching careers in Japan, and venture into a life of full-time travel.

1) Where have you travelled with just a carry-on?

We have travelled for the past ten years with only a carry-on bag each, as well as a smaller daypack, to many countries in Europe and Asia. Our longest stint was a ten-week trip from Japan to New Zealand and the southern US. We had to pack for multiple climates, which was a bit of a challenge.

2) What are the advantages and disadvantages of travelling with a carry-on? Do you think it's worth it?

The advantages, for us, far outweigh the disadvantages, and it's so very worth it.

A nice financial advantage, besides avoiding baggage check-in fees for budget airlines, is if the airline needs volunteers to be "bumped" to a later flight, we can easily volunteer since the airline doesn't have to hunt our bags down.

As for disadvantages, there are only a few. After checking in at the airport, we have our carry-on plus a daypack to contend with while waiting for our flight. We usually remedy this by heading directly to our gate's waiting area, finding a comfy spot to park our carry-ons, and taking turns "babysitting the bags" while the other goes off for a walk or to find something to eat.

3) What luggage do you use and what do you like or not like about it?

I use a JanSport Cargo Hold 22-inch roller bag, and I love it because it has two corner-mounted oversize 5-inch wheels that are much more rugged than the smaller wheels on most bags. It handles beautifully on uneven, cobblestone streets in Italy or on muddy dirt roads in Cambodia because the bigger wheels raise the bag off the ground.

My husband uses the Travelpro T-Pro Bold luggage system. He has the rolling carry-on and the matching smaller daypack. He loves his luggage and especially the daypack because it has a strap that slips easily over the telescoping handle of his roller bag and secures it on top, so he doesn't have to wear the daypack all the time.

All of our bags are a darker "army green" colour because we have found that this is the best colour to camouflage the dirt and grime that happens when travelling, especially in developing countries.

4) Do you travel with a day bag in addition to your main carry-on?

The daypack I use is a Jeep foldaway backpack. It is as light as a feather, somewhat water resistant, and folds into its own pouch about the size of a makeup bag. That makes it simple to tuck inside my roller bag if the flight limits us to just one bag. And it holds a lot of stuff for such a small, lightweight bag.

5) What clothes and shoes do you travel with? Are there any particular brands or fabrics that you recommend?

I strongly believe in the benefit of travelling with a capsule wardrobe of a few basic pieces that can be mixed, matched, and layered to create many different outfits. I stick to a basic colour palette of black, heather grey, purple, and teal. People often ask if I get bored with wearing only a capsule wardrobe, but I really don't find that I do. It was way more overwhelming for me to decide what to wear when I used to travel with two dozen tops and bottoms and had to dig something out from the bottom of an overstuffed suitcase, only to find that it needed ironing before I could wear it.

With my capsule collection, I simply change my look by adding an accessory like a cute scarf, jean jacket, or cardigan, and that keeps me interested.

When travelling, we mostly wear light cotton or synthetic, moisture wicking fibres that are breathable. I like to employ the "touch test" before buying anything. If it doesn't feel soft and lightweight, it simply doesn't make the cut. Old Navy brand t-shirts, tank tops, and camisoles tend to pass my touch test with flying colours. Their stuff is super soft, has an attractive feminine fit, and holds up to many washes pretty well.

As for underwear, I usually wear my Fiona sports bra by Moving Comfort, while my dressier Victoria's Secret bra is packed away, and the panties I use exclusively are seamless "no show" Wacoal boy-cut bikini bottoms. I love them because they don't show panty lines, wash and dry in a flash, and still look cute, rather than "granny-like."

I travel with a pair of walking shoes (dark denim Converse low tops), silver-grey ballet flats, a nude dressier flat sandal, and a pair of black-and-silver flip-flops that can be dressed up or down. My Keen brand hiking boots are what I wear to cold weather destinations. All are cute and comfortable, with some form of arch support whenever possible. I use cushioned insoles with my Converse to keep them comfortable for longer walks. Scaling down my shoes was my biggest challenge in long-term travel, but I am quite content with my selection now. This, coming from a former shoe addict who had over 40 pairs of shoes and boots crammed into my overstuffed closet at home!

6) How do you manage the liquids rule on flights?

I use a quart plastic baggie with travel-size contact solution, facial moisturiser, travel-size hairspray, a tiny tube of toothpaste, and my daily liquid foundation with SPF sun protection. To keep from having too many liquids, I use cloth makeup remover wipes rather than liquid toner.

When we arrive at our destination, we first look to see what the hotel may have available before heading out to buy things like mouthwash, sunscreen, toothpaste, or shampoo to use during our stay.

7) What technology do you pack?

I have my iPad and a small Sony Cyber-shot G series camera. Randy has his Sony Vaio Pro 13-inch super lightweight laptop, extra portable 1 TB hard drive, and 8 GB flash drive to store our important files. Everything is backed up on our Google Drive. We each have a small flip-phone (no iPhones for us) with SIM cards we purchase on arrival in each country.

8) Do you travel with any luxury items?

We have streamlined our packing over the years, but I still manage to drag along my electric InStyler hot brush. It is rather bulky and a bit of an inconvenience to make space for, but I haven't been able to leave it behind yet because my hair is a frizzy mess without it.

9) Did you pack anything that you regretted or got rid of?

I have found that packing pyjamas is a waste of space. I got rid of them and am now using soft leggings and camisoles as my pyjamas so they can be used during the day sometimes as an extra layer as well as at night.

You can follow Lori and Randy's travels on their blog, Freetirement.

19. Alexandra Jimenez - The Stylish Traveller

Alex has been travelling around the world since 2008 and manages to pack light while staying stylish. She runs Travel Fashion Girl, the ultimate women's travel resource for packing, fashion, and beauty.

1) Where have you travelled with just a carry-on?

I've been travelling carry-on only full-time since 2013, including eight months in Southeast Asia in 2013; eight months through Egypt and Southeast Asia in 2014; two weeks in Paris and Italy in 2014; and four months in India, Sri Lanka, and Southeast Asia in 2015. Can you tell I like Southeast Asia?

2) What luggage do you use and what do you like or not like about it?

For a backpack, the Osprey Farpoint 55 (40 main pack + 15 daypack) is amazing. It's super lightweight with lockable zippers, durable materials, and an easy to organise space—with packing organisers of course!

I'm suffering from back issues and decided to make the move to wheels: the Osprey Ozone 22", which I love. It's like the Farpoint backpack but with wheels! One of the most important features in wheeled luggage for me as a long-term traveller is ultra-durable rugged wheels I can drag through gravel, broken pavement, and up steps without worrying that my bag is going to fall apart. That's why I travel with this brand and not a regular wheeled suitcase with wheels that are made for smooth sidewalks.

3) Do you travel with a day bag in addition to your main carry-on?

Yes, I have my day bag for my laptop, passport, and money. Technically everything fits in my main suitcase, but for security and convenience, I have my valuables separate.

4) Is it possible to look stylish when travelling with a carry-on? How do you manage it?

I suppose it's possible to look stylish rather than fashion forward. I feel style is about what makes you feel confident and fashion is following trends.

As a long-term traveller, I've worked hard to narrow down my personal style and the pieces that are most flattering to me. In my twenties, I played more with fashion, so I liked having more clothing, but now in my early thirties, I'm enjoying developing my own signature style and don't need as much stuff.

I don't have a problem spending money on the few clothes I do have because I'll wear them all the time. More importantly, I want to wear what makes me feel good even if the price tag is higher.

5) What clothes and shoes do you travel with? Are there any particular brands or fabrics that you recommend?

Clothes are based on where I'm going and the weather. My personal colour favourites are black, white, royal blue, vivid green, and the occasional red hue. I had a colour assessment and learned what colours work best for me, narrowing down my choices further.

I don't travel with a particular brand. I like Athleta, Adea, and Anatomie for technical travel clothes like basic tops and pants, but the rest is from Topshop, H&M, or local brands wherever I am.

Shoes are always difficult, but I have two styles I always gravitate toward: sandals by the beach and boots in the cold as my primary footwear. I pack super lightweight trainers for the odd hike. And my third pair of shoes is something I can walk in for hours. In the cold this is boots with gel inserts and in the heat it's Birkenstocks.

6) Have you travelled in cold weather and how did you pack for it?

In the cold, fabrics are what matter most, and I drop the cash for awesome merino wool or silk thermals. If you have these under everything, you'll be much warmer. I also try to choose lightweight but very warm sweaters in merino wool and cashmere, so I get the double dose of warm fabrics!

7) What makeup and beauty products do you travel with? How do you manage the liquids rule on flights?

I buy liquids as I go and don't usually travel with full-size toiletries. I watched how much shampoo I used, and a 90 ml (3 oz) bottle lasts me weeks (unless I'm diving constantly). I also decant things like foundation, which I hardly use, and instead of travelling with a massive glass bottle, I just have a little of the product for that odd day when I want to turn it up a notch.

For makeup, I have a four-shadow makeup palette, eyeliner, lip gloss, mascara, blush, a tube of concealer, NARS The Multiple for a healthy glow, and 50 ml of foundation. On a day-to-day basis, if I do wear makeup it consists of mascara, NARS, blush, and concealer.

8) What technology do you pack?

Too much, but I need it to keep my website going: MacBook Air, MiFi device, portable charger, smartphone, point-and-shoot camera, underwater housing for the camera, memory cards, memory card reader (for the laptop), scuba diving watch, portable memory drive, and I think that's it.

9) Did you pack anything that you regretted or got rid of?

Not anymore. My biggest regret is packing clothes I hated just because I thought that's what travellers should wear, but it's not the brand that matters, it's the functionality.

10) Do you have any other tips for packing light?

Plan, research, and choose functional clothing that you actually like. At least, this goes for women. For guys, try to be aware that you have to wear your shirt with your shorts/trousers, so don't go overboard with prints.

Choose light luggage because if your bag weighs 4 kg (9 lb), then there goes most of your baggage allowance. 2 kg (4.4 lb) is a good maximum.

The main thing is to get packing cubes and organisers. They're a game changer.

You can read Alex's packing tips at Travel Fashion Girl.

20. Lucy Sheref - The Makeup Lover

Lucy (aka WanderLuce) is a beauty blogger and London native who has been travelling with her impressively bearded boyfriend since January 2014. She has a passion for seeing the world while keeping her favourite lipstick on.

1) Where have you travelled with just a carry-on?

I have been travelling with a carry-on for about six months. (I travelled with a 70L Berghaus backpack for most of 2014.) I have been to Indonesia, Thailand, Malaysia and Singapore with a 30L carry-on, and I've never been happier with my new packing style. I'd always admired other travellers who have successfully travelled with carry-on only, especially Erin and Simon, but as a beauty product junkie, I never thought I could do it. However if I can, anyone can!

2) What are the advantages and disadvantages of travelling with a carry-on? Do you think it's worth it?

Most people pack about a third too much stuff, whether they are going on a two-week or two-month trip. Having a smaller backpack automatically makes you think about everything you bring: "Is it worth it? Do I really need it?" Travelling with a carry-on means you have to be strict with yourself, so I never make impulse purchases and follow a pretty strict "one in, one out" rule.

There can be disadvantages, though, like never being able to bring your toiletries from home, which for me can be a pain as toiletries in Asia are pricey in comparison to the UK. I've become creative about packing, so it's not something that would make me change my style.

3) What luggage do you use and what do you like or not like about it?

I use a Karrimor Trail 35-litre backpack, which was about £16 ($26) on sale, and I love it! It's a traditional top-loading style, so you do have to be organised, but I prefer this style as it's so comfortable to wear. It's really sturdy and has a built-in rain cover, which is incredibly useful, especially in rainy season.

4) Do you travel with a day bag in addition to your main carry-on?

No, but I do have an awesome canvas tote, which folds up small so I can pack it in my backpack when I travel. We mostly stay places for more than a few weeks, so I tend to use it when we are settled. I chuck my camera, SPF, and water in it...and my Arden Eight Hour cream.

5) You're a beauty blogger, so you obviously love your products. What cosmetics and toiletries do you pack and how do you get around the liquids rule on flights?

It always surprises people how little I pack in the way of liquids. I use solid shampoo, soap, and sunblock bars from Lush, which are amazing. I really rely on Lush and happily there is a branch in Bangkok, so I can stock up if I need to. Lush does offer solid conditioner bars; however, I wouldn't recommend them for anyone who has thick, curly hair, like me, as they are hard to work with and don't give you the level of moisture you need. I pack a hair mask or intensive leave-in conditioner instead so that I can get away with a much smaller size.

SPF is super important, and if you have ever travelled to Asia you'll know how tricky it can be to get something decent for a good price, so along with my Lush solid sunblock, I take a Sisley SPF Face Stick (30 ml/1 oz), which lasts for ages (although it should, as it's very pricey!).

I take a few face mask sachets too, which are really lightweight and fit easily in my TSA-approved bag. I am never without my Eight Hour Cream; it multitasks as a moisturiser for anywhere super dry—be it your elbows, lips, or even the ends of your hair.

I have a small makeup bag—it's a Liberty waterproof one, so it's pretty and practical—and I pack seven products: 30 ml Clinique Even Better foundation, which is SPF15 and oil-free; a slimline Sleek palette with bronze, blush, and highlighter; a miniature mascara sample; Kat Von D eyeliner; MAC Costa Chic lipstick; Lancome Velours lip lacquer; and an Essie nail polish (normally Mint Candy Apple). Multitasking is the name of the game!

6) Is it possible to be stylish and pack light? What clothes and shoes do you travel with?

Absolutely! I find the key is sticking to a colour palette and taking things that will multitask. I mostly wear black, white, and grey, with some stripes/floral, which means that everything I pack goes together.

I'm a big fan of Kristin from Be My Travel Muse and Alex from Travel Fashion Girl, who are both super-stylish travellers who only take a carry-on, and I often check out their packing lists for inspiration by country.

Because I tend to travel to hot countries, I only need three pairs of shoes: trainers, flip-flops, and a nicer pair of sandals/espadrilles. If I were to travel to different climates, it might be a little harder.

My hardest working item of clothing is my black flippy skirt. Denim shorts and simple tank tops are also staples, and I cannot live without my black jersey peg trousers, which are super comfy, stylish, and perfect for long journeys, as they feel like pyjamas. (Note: not Ali Baba/harem trousers, which suit nobody!)

Something I picked up from the website Her Packing List is to take a sports bra. I do work out when I'm travelling, but I also use it on bus/train/plane journeys when underwire is not a comfortable option.

7) Have you travelled in cold weather and how did you pack for it?

Only Darjeeling in India, but that was incredibly cold! In colder weather I'll pack more lightweight sweaters and a few pairs of tights to wear with summer dresses (yep, it works!), as well as lots of leggings that I can double up on to keep really warm.

Uniqlo's HeatTech range is amazing. Leggings and tops made from super thin heat-retaining fabric—basically they're thermals. I love my thermals, and picking up mittens/scarves/woolly hats, etc. are often pretty cheap en route. In Darjeeling, travellers are often heading off on a big trek, so warm clothing was readily available.

8) What technology do you pack?

Because I work on the road, I pack a fair amount of technology, which I need to review as it's far too bulky. I take a 13-inch MacBook Pro, Canon EOS 1200 DSLR, unlocked iPhone 4s, small external hard drive (Western Digital My Passport), and a Canon PowerShot point-and-shoot digital camera. Oh, and all the chargers! They do all fit, but I have to carry my DSLR around my neck, which isn't ideal. I have toyed with the idea of selling it and switching to using my point-and-shoot, but I'm just not ready yet!

9) Do you travel with any luxury items?

I guess my excess of makeup/skincare could be considered non-essential, but I truly have cut it down a lot over the past couple of years, and I think it's a fairly tight edit now.

We take snorkels with us everywhere, which actually isn't necessary, but because we are both such water babies (Oli is training to be a dive instructor), we felt it was important to have them for practicality as well as saving a bit of money.

We also take Yorkshire tea bags, which is definitely our little luxury, but we love our tea and will never compromise! Everyone who comes to visit has to bring us more. We often get laughed at for playing up to the English stereotype, but when you're thousands of miles from home and having a little low moment, there's nothing nicer than a proper brew.

You can follow Lucy's travels at Wanderluce.

21. Jade Johnston - The Family with a Toddler

Jade travels the world with her husband and young son. She blogs about budget and family travel at Our Oyster.

1) Where have you travelled with just a carry-on?

I try to travel carry-on only whenever possible. Most recently we went to Indonesia for two weeks with a toddler and only two carry-on bags. We generally only travel carry-on only to warm destinations and on short trips.

2) Is travelling carry-on only with a toddler really possible? How do you manage it?

Travelling carry-on only with a toddler is definitely possible. And when you consider that one entire carry-on bag that we take with us is full of camera equipment, it becomes even more feasible for someone not packing 10 kg of camera kit.

Our toddler is still in diapers, but you can buy those anywhere in the world, so we only pack enough for the flight and our first day. His clothes pack down extremely small, and we only bring a couple of toys with us, so his luggage doesn't take up much space at all.

Luckily, babies and toddlers get free checked luggage for strollers and car seats. If your stroller has any pockets or storage, take advantage of that. The stroller always has to be checked, but every airline is different. They either make you check it when you check in all your luggage, or they take it from you at boarding and put it under the plane.

3) What luggage do you use and what do you like or not like about it?

Our most recent addition, which we really love, is the Eagle Creek Morphus 22. There is a section with wheels and a backpack that attaches to it. You can use it as one bag or separate the two and have two carry-on bags.

Another great bag we use is called the Rolo. This is like a giant toiletry bag—you pack your clothes into the different compartments, and then roll the bag up into a tube and tighten the straps. I packed a week's worth of clothes in here for Jacob and me, and it was small enough when rolled up that we managed to take it on a flight as the "additional" item.

Because we travel with a fair amount of professional camera gear, a good camera bag is a must. We have trialled a few different bags, but so far the Kata 33 DL is our favourite.

4) Do you travel with a day bag in addition to your main carry-on?

Now that we use the Morphus 22, it comes with a day bag that you can separate from the bag. We often use the storage on the stroller instead of taking a separate day bag.

5) How do you manage the liquids rule on flights?

Since we still travel with a stroller, I usually pack any of the liquids that are oversize in the stroller storage compartment. The only things I have trouble buying in small amounts are contact solution and special products for my hair. But most other things you can get in small amounts or just buy at your destination.

6) What technology do you pack?

We pack a lot of technology.

Camera gear: Canon 6D, Tamron 24-70 mm lens, Canon 6D battery pack, Tamron 150-600 mm lens, Sigma 105 mm lens, tripod.

Technology: Samsung Note 4, MacBook Pro, Samsung tablet (for Jacob).

We don't always take the telephoto lens, but we make sure to have it if we will be doing any wildlife photography.

7) Are there any other items you recommend specifically for travelling with a toddler?

We don't go anywhere without the tablet loaded up with his favourite shows and cartoons. Dora the Explorer has placated him on many a flight!

8) Do you have any other tips for packing light?

One thing that I try to eliminate from my luggage is a towel. Towels are bulky and don't dry quickly. If we are staying in guesthouses and hotels, we won't bring one, as they are usually provided. Sometimes you just have to pack a towel, though. I have found that using a sarong as a towel is a great solution because it dries very quickly, packs down small, and can also be used as a skirt or cover up at the beach.

You can follow Jade and her family's travels at Our Oyster.

22. John Farnsworth - The Artist

John is an artist, photographer, and blogger who sketches and paints on his travels. He is in his 70s and is based in New Mexico during the summer and travels solo in the winter.

1) Where have you travelled with just a carry-on?

England, France, Spain, Italy, Switzerland, Argentina, Peru, Mexico, and the United States, from a few days to three months.

2) What luggage do you use and what do you like or not like about it?

I use an Olympia Sports Plus 18" rolling backpack. I've been using it since 2005, and it has served me well on three continents. I have tried others, but none has given me the flexibility of this bag.

It's lightweight and the padded, hidden backpack straps and waistband come in handy when confronted with cobblestones, crowded sidewalks, high kerbs, mud, etc., or when I need my hands free to photograph or sketch. It fits easily into the overhead bins on aeroplanes and is less obvious when checking in.

I do wish it had four wheels, as it is so much easier to walk alongside a bag for long distances than to bear the weight while pulling it along.

3) Do you travel with a day bag in addition to your main carry-on?

Yes, I have two options, depending on the weather and what I plan on doing on a given day.

I have an over-the-shoulder or across-the-chest Everest utility bag. In it I carry my iPad Air, iPhone 6 Plus, camera, charger, cables, accessories, and passport.

Alternatively, I wear a SCOTTeVEST, in which I carry the same items plus, if painting, a small watercolour or oil colour palette, paper, brushes, pens, and pencil.

On my most recent trip to Mexico, I purchased an inexpensive, woven, lightweight backpack. It proved to be very convenient for carrying my jacket and vest in warmer weather.

4) Is it difficult to be a travelling artist? What art supplies do you travel with?

Because I use what I call my (Un)Limited Palette, consisting of only the three primary colours plus white and use walnut oil as my medium so there are no solvents to deal with, and because I restrict the size of my work to 12 x 16 inches or smaller when travelling, travelling solo is not too difficult.

My oil palette is a 3.5 x 7 x 1.25 inch plastic box, and, with three or four small brushes, paper, and a small backup box of oils, I'm good to go for a month or more.

My watercolour palette is a small tin one from Sennelier, measuring 2.75 x 4.75 x 0.75 inches when closed. My brushes are small, made for travel, and some even have water reservoirs in their handles. Some paper, three tubes of backup watercolour, and, again, I'm ready for a month or more.

When teaching workshops, I have to carry more materials than when travelling alone. My new woven Mexican bag should accommodate everything needed for any upcoming workshops. I'll just have to wear the vest and either wear the jacket too or carry it over my free arm.

If that isn't enough, for instance if I'm supplying materials for everyone in the class, I will ship the necessary materials ahead.

When travelling, I paint oils on paper, usually 6 x 6 or 5 x 7 inches. Watercolours are generally 6 x 9 inches. If I decide to work larger, say 9 x 12 or 12 x 16, I will carry blocks or pads of paper in my woven Mexican bag.

On my most recent trip, however, despite carrying a complete watercolour setup, I ended up sketching with only my finger on either my iPhone 6 Plus or iPad Air.

5) What technology do you pack?

- Folding power strip from Staples, with three outlets and two USB ports
- CE Travel Universal Adapter/surge protector cube
- PNY 128 GB thumb drive
- iPad Air 128 GB Wi-Fi and cellular with a soft silicone cover
- Bracketron iTilt desktop stand
- iPhone 6 Plus
- iPhone 4s
- 3 Apple chargers and cables
- Earbuds
- Mini tripod + Joby GripTight Mount
- Panasonic Lumix TZ40 camera with 20x optical zoom
- Panasonic charger
- USB cable
- 4 batteries
- Several memory cards
- Card reader
- Screen cleaning cloth

6) What clothes and shoes do you travel with? Are there any particular brands or fabrics that you recommend?

I wear jeans, a belt, a t-shirt, a shirt, a sports jacket and/or SCOTTeVEST, and Blundstone boots.

I pack:

- Travelsmith pants (These nylon pants are no longer available.)
- 2 t-shirts
- 2 shirts
- Underwear
- Shorts
- Socks
- Cloth flat cap
- REI merino wool buff
- Merino wool sweater vest
- Silk aviator scarf

7) Did you pack anything that you regretted or got rid of?

Over the years, a lot!

Recently? Umbrella, suspenders, thick sole flip-flops, pillowcase, notebooks, excess art supplies and equipment, and a tripod. (I've been carrying a tripod but haven't used it since 2005! Considering a monopod, but probably wouldn't use it, either.)

8) Do you have any other tips for packing light?

I have a light elastic cord with one of those squeeze-to-slide adjusters that worked great for keeping my Mexican woven bag tight against the handle of my rolling bag, while a carabiner made for a quick way to attach and release its straps to the top of the handle.

Carabiners and rubber bands are always good to have on hand for unexpected uses.

Toilet paper. Remove the tube from a half-used roll and you have a very compact, carry-anywhere emergency supply. (I also use it for cleaning my brushes when painting.)

You can enjoy John's artwork at A Farnsworth a Day.

23. Brigid and Dan Mossop - The Long-Term Travellers

Brigid and Dan spent a year travelling through Latin America before falling in love with Bolivia and settling down in the White City of Sucre for five months. While they've moved on for the time being, their hearts are still somewhere in the altiplano, and they continue to share their experiences of this fantastic country at Bolivian Life.

1) Where have you travelled with just a carry-on?

Dan and I travelled with a carry-on for two years through Latin America, starting in Mexico and finishing in Chile.

2) What luggage do you use and what do you like or not like about it?

We use 30L Kathmandu backpacks we bought back in Australia. Dan and I love that these backpacks have lots of different compartments to store important documents and keep our valuables hidden. The padded back pocket is great for storing our laptops, keeping them safe from bumpy bus rides and general wear and tear from travelling.

3) Do you travel with a day bag in addition to your main carry-on?

Yes. Dan travels with a small daypack and me with a small handbag.

4) What clothes and shoes do you travel with? Are there any particular brands or fabrics that you recommend?

We like to buy base layers made from fabrics that breathe to manage moisture, middle layers of fleece and wool to provide insulation, and outer layers such as a windbreaker to protect against the elements. Long trousers and sleeves are a good choice for the tropical regions to protect against infectious insect bites.

This was my complete clothing packing list for the trip:

- Jeans/trousers
- Exercise pants
- Leggings
- Skirt
- Shorts
- Nighttime outfit
- Fleece jacket
- Hoodie
- Cardigan
- 2 long-sleeve tops
- 2 short-sleeve t-shirts
- 2 tank tops
- Rain jacket
- Pyjamas
- Swimmers
- Sarong
- 2 bras
- 7 underwear
- 4 pairs socks + 1 thick pair for nighttime
- Flip-flops
- Runners
- Ballet flats

5) What technology do you pack?

We packed the following technology:

- 2 iPhones - We used our phones as a camera and music player.
- 2 laptops and 1 tablet - We travelled with 11-inch HP laptops, which were great for working online, and the iPad, which was handy for watching movies, reading books, and Skyping home.
- 2 headphones
- Laptop and phone chargers
- Adapters
- USB
- External battery pack - One of our favourite purchases. Having an external battery was great for working in cafes and keeping our electronics charged on the go.

6) Do you travel with any luxury items?

It's not safe to drink the water in many Latin American countries, which is why we packed a SteriPEN. We could have purchased bottled water during our travels, however, constantly drinking out of plastic bottles is not only terrible for the environment, but also eats into your travel budget over time. The SteriPEN, though a little expensive upfront, was a win-win solution.

7) Did you pack anything that you regretted or got rid of?

I initially packed a pair of high heels, which I discarded one month into the trip. After wearing them a grand total of once, I just couldn't justify taking up valuable space in my backpack for something I would use so infrequently. While I think it's possible to achieve both style and comfort while travelling, in order to pack light you have to be smart and selective about the clothing items you bring with you.

8) How do you organise your things in your luggage?

We packed our clothes into plastic snap bags. Not only did this help to keep our clothes organised, but protected them from spillages and wet weather. We also rolled our clothes instead of folding them, taking up less space in our backpacks and keeping our clothes wrinkle-free.

You can see Brigid and Dan's packing list and read their Bolivia travel tips at

Bolivian Life.

24. Patrick Schroeder - The Camper

Patrick has been travelling around the world since 2007, usually by bicycle or on foot, with the goal to visit every country. (He has visited 70% so far.)

1) Where have you travelled with just a carry-on?

Some examples: Ireland, two weeks. Tunisia, five weeks. The Canaries, two weeks. Southeast Asia, five months. West Africa, three months.

2) What luggage do you use and what do you like or not like about it?

I use a very light backpack designed for adventure races. Unnecessary accessories, straps, etc. I cut off to save weight. This is done because I often cover my distance by muscle power, either hiking or biking, and want to preserve energy. The current one I use is a 26L Jack Wolfskin Ascent pack, just below 500 g (1.1 lb) after removing parts I do not need. There are lighter alternatives, but this one was the best value for money.

Items I take:

- 2 pairs of socks
- 1 pair of shoes
- 2-3 pairs of underwear
- 1 long-sleeve shirt

- 1 windbreaker
- 1 zip-off trouser
- 1 buff (doubles as a towel)
- 1 long-sleeve fleece
- 1 baseball cap
- 1 watch

Most of this you wear on your body, so the backpack is still empty.

Add to it a tent, sleeping bag, and mattress, which together take up about 6 litres of volume and 2 kg (4.4 lb) of weight. Then documents, passport, money, some electronics, smartphone, e-book reader, head torch, camera in a net bag, and my backpack is half full. The rest of the space remains empty, available for food and water, for which I might carry a water bladder, usually a Platypus 2L or a Deuter Source 2L.

The backpack has two net bags on its sides, for a bottle and some snacks.

3) Do you travel with a day bag in addition to your main carry-on?

No, my main carry-on is light enough to be worn all day.

4) You've managed to pack for camping trips in your hand luggage. How do you get around the airline restrictions on items like a penknife and camping stove fuel?

I take neither penknife nor camping stove fuel. Nor camping stove for that matter. As a knife I use a titanium folding butter knife by Nordisk—small, light, and blunt. You can still cut bread and spread peanut butter, but the tip is round. No airline has commented on it so far.

I eat a lot of trail food, sandwiches, muesli, etc. and do not cook. This is a conscious decision and has nothing to do with the inability to check in a stove or not. I travelled 18 months by bike once, carrying a stove, using it twice. I just don't need it. For people that do take one, I recommend checking out Zen Stoves and just leaving out the fuel. These stoves weigh about 150 g (5 oz) and use alcohol as fuel, which you can buy in almost any supermarket or pharmacy.

5) What camping gear do you recommend for packing light?

I'm averse to suggesting camping gear for its weight. First and foremost it should be adequate for the climate you face; then you can worry about its weight. I own a Helsport Ringstind Superlight tent (less than 1 kg/2.2 lb), several sleeping bags which weigh less than 1 kg (2.2 lb), and a Thermarest NeoAir Xlite clocking in at 350 g (12 oz). The best sleeping bags I can recommend are Yeti VIB or Passion series. This means you have a complete camping setup for just below 2 kg (4.4 lb).

I take no cooking gear, but an alcohol stove and fuel and a titanium mug to make coffee, tea, soup, or noodles, would add another 200-300 g (7-10 oz).

6) What clothes and shoes do you travel with? Are there any particular brands or fabrics that you recommend?

I heartily recommend merino wool. Any brand is fine; personally, I own items from Icebreaker, Ortovox, and SmartWool. They are perfect as a base layer. For shoes, I prefer light running shoes or flip-flops.

For a seriously in-depth explanation of hiking/travel clothing, check out Andrew Skurka's 13 essential clothing items.

7) How do you organise your things in your luggage?

I use a net bag for the electronics and a small dry bag for clothing, which also doubles as a pillow. Netbook and e-book reader go into the large pocket at the back of the backpack. Items I use often or might need quickly, like the head torch, money, or notebook, are at the top in the cover, easily reachable.

8) Do you have any other tips for packing light?

I only take one or two sets of clothing with me, all of it quick dry. I wash it in the evening and wear it the next morning. There is no need for two identical trousers or two t-shirts. Every piece I take fills a specific role—for example, one merino base layer, one fleece, and one windbreaker. These are three long-sleeve tops, but all offer different uses.

You can follow Patrick's travels at World Bicyclist.

25. Jenny and Tom Krones - The Digital Nomad Couple

Tom and Jenny are originally from California, but can usually be found a lot closer to the equatorial belt. They started an app development company on the road and have been calling anywhere with an internet connection "the home office" for the last four years. They write about their travels at Till the Money Runs Out.

1) Where have you travelled with just a carry-on?

We have been location independent for four years, and so it is difficult to determine when a "trip" ends and begins. We have been travelling for the majority of that time with carry-on-size luggage and have visited South America, Central America, Europe, Southeast Asia, Australia, and North America.

2) What luggage do you use and what do you like or not like about it?

I use the Osprey Farpoint 40 and Tom has the Tortuga Backpack. We switched to these bags about six months ago and so far we really like them. They both have laptop sleeves, which is the main difference from our previous bags and a total lifesaver.

Tom feels like his bag is "too blocky," and I am not a fan of the net water bottle sleeves on the outside of mine. I also wish the Osprey was a little taller and thinner as it feels a little wide for me, but other than that they are darn near perfect!

3) Do you travel with a day bag in addition to your main carry-on?

We travel with one REI Flashpack (18L) that I pack inside my backpack on travel days. It has all the features I wanted—it takes a hydration pouch for long hikes and fits both of our computers for going to a coffee shop to work—and folds up really small to fit into my regular bag.

4) What clothes and shoes do you travel with? Are there any particular brands or fabrics that you recommend?

It is important to both of us to travel with "regular-looking" clothes. When we first started our trip, we had more "technical" gear, like pants that zip off into shorts and things like that. I felt really self-conscious and weird every time I wore them, and after a few months, we drastically changed our approach. Now we travel with clothes that travel well, but don't look like travel clothes.

I was recently introduced to Athleta (thanks, Erin!) and I really like their skirts. They have pockets, built-in shorts, are stretchy, and look pretty cute, but I could also climb a tree in them if I wanted.

My other favourite item is a lightweight, button-up long-sleeve shirt that I can use to cover up from the sun, layer in the cold, or wear to nice dinners. Tom loves shorts or pants that have extra zippered pockets that are near impossible to pickpocket.

5) How do you manage the liquids rule on flights?

I am not advising that anyone else does this, but I really just don't sweat it, and so far nothing has happened. Meaning that I often will have a toothpaste tube or sunblock bottle in my bag that is over 100 ml, and I don't bother pulling it out and putting it in the zip-lock baggies that airport security is so keen on, and I have never been stopped. On that note, in over four years, I have never separated my liquids when we go through security, and no one has ever said anything.

6) What technology do you pack?

Between the two of us we have:

- MacBook Air 13-inch + charger
- MacBook Pro Retina 13-inch + charger
- Amazon Kindle Paperwhite
- iPhone 6 64 GB unlocked
- iPad Mini Wi-Fi 16 GB
- 2 x 1 TB external hard drives
- Mini power strip
- 2 to 3 prong converter
- USB flash drive
- Canon EOS Rebel SL1 digital SLR camera
- Canon EF-S 55-250 mm F4-5.6 lens
- Canon EF-S 24 mm f/2.8 lens
- Camera battery charger + 2 batteries
- 2 SanDisk Extreme 32 GB micro SD cards
- 4 GB SD card (generic back-up card)
- GoPro HERO4 SILVER
- Cheap flexi-leg mini tripod
- SteriPEN (USB chargeable)
- Array of USB cables (Kindle, GoPro, Sonicare, lightning cables)
- Anker Astro mini external battery power bank
- 2 headphones
- Headphone splitter
- Alfa Long-Range Dual-Band Wireless USB for Extreme Distance Connections
- Sonicare toothbrush with two heads and USB chargeable case

7) Do you travel with any luxury items?

Tom travels with a full-size feather pillow, and I travel with a ton of accessories (big earrings, rings, necklaces, etc.). I probably travel with too many clothes, but they all get so darn small when I put them in a packing cube or vacuum bag that there is nothing stopping me. Our Sonicare toothbrush is also probably a luxury item as it takes up more space than regular toothbrushes. We never know when our next dental cleaning will be, so we like to have it.

8) Did you pack anything that you regretted or got rid of?

We used to travel with a double hammock, travel towels, a mosquito net, and more technical style clothes, such as pants that zipped off into shorts. We only used the hammock once; we have found that if we are in a place where we need a mosquito net around the bed, it will be provided; and we always stay in places where towels are provided. So we stopped travelling with all of those things.

9) Do you have any other tips for packing light?

Our number one tip is to make the choice and pick a small bag. It's simple math and human nature; your stuff will expand to fit exactly into whatever size bag you have. Get your bag first and then start picking what you want to bring. If you make a huge pile of stuff you'd like to take, the small bag will be more intimidating, but if you commit to a small bag from the start, you will make it work.

We see people all the time lugging around 70L bags. It looks like it hurts.

You can read Tom and Jenny's packing list for four months in Mexico and follow their travels at Till the Money Runs Out.

26. David Danzeiser - The Solo Traveller

David spent a year travelling solo around the world and is now pursuing his goal of becoming location independent so he can continue travelling full-time.

1) Where have you travelled with just a carry-on?

At the end of 2012, I took a year-long trip around the world out of a 26-litre backpack to 23 countries in Australia, Asia, Africa, the Middle East, Europe, and South America.

I continue to live out of the same backpack and have travelled around the US doing various road trips and smaller trips, as well as living in Mexico. So in total about two and a half years.

2) What luggage do you use and what do you like or not like about it?

I use Tom Bihn's 26L Smart Alec, with some added internal organiser pouches (also by Tom Bihn but sold separately).

Likes:

Great organisation - The bag itself has great organisation, but Tom Bihn also sells separate pouches for added organisation. Each bag has o-rings throughout the bag to hook the accessories into.

Inconspicuous - You can get bags in plain colours (mine is all black) so you don't stick out as a backpacker.

Durable - It's made out of cordura fabric, so it's built to take a beating.

Dislikes:

Not waterproof - It's water resistant, which is nice, but I'd love it if it were completely waterproof.

Non-odour resistant straps - I found after a year that the straps, in particular, were smelling pretty rancid.

3) Do you travel with a day bag in addition to your main carry-on?

The bag itself is small enough to act as a day bag. I did purchase a reusable grocery bag to carry food when I'm travelling in expensive countries. I use the grocery bag to store unnecessary items when I take the bag out on day hikes.

4) What clothes and shoes do you travel with? Are there any particular brands or fabrics that you recommend?

I highly recommend any clothing made of merino wool. It's great for keeping you warm when it's cold and cool when it's hot. It dries super quickly and is extremely odour resistant. The brand I wear the most is Icebreaker. My favourite underwear is ExOfficio, and my socks are Darn Tough brand.

5) What technology do you pack?

Professional camera (Nikon D5300), iPhone 6, Sony Vaio laptop, Amazon Kindle, external hard drive, Fitbit, and accompanying chargers/cables.

6) Do you travel with any luxury items?

Pretty much all the technology is a luxury; all I'd really need would be the iPhone 6. I also carry a tripod and a large journal, which I don't really need.

7) Did you pack anything that you regretted or got rid of?

Travel clothesline, compact flashlight, waterproof/rugged camera, long underwear, sandals, silk travel liner.

8) How do you organise your things in your luggage?

I keep things I use often, like my camera and journal, in the reusable grocery bag. Toiletries, clean undies, and socks are kept near the top of the bag. Charging cables are kept together in side pockets along with my water bottle.

9) Do you have any other tips for packing light?

My biggest tip is to cut down on clothing. If you're travelling long-term, you're going to need to do laundry anyway, so at most you should have enough for a week. Buy clothing that is compact and quick drying, and stay away from bulky accessories like overcoats you'll rarely wear.

I highly recommend an insulated water bottle. Not only will you reduce your waste of plastic bottles, but there's nothing better than being out on a hot day and having an ice-cold beverage to drink all day and vice versa when it's cold outside.

I also recommend a compact travel towel. I use the Packtowl Ultralite XL.

You can read David's packing list and follow his travels at The Quest for Awesome.

27. Nora Dunn - The Professional Hobo

Nora is The Professional Hobo; a Canadian who sold everything she owned in 2006 (including a busy financial planning practice) to embrace her dreams of full-time travel. She's been on the road ever since, working as a freelance writer and teaching people how to travel full-time in a financially sustainable way.

1) Where have you travelled with just a carry-on?

When I started travelling full-time in 2007, I did so with one checked bag (into which everything I owned fit). In 2010, I started leaving the checked bag behind and travelled with carry-on only for up to three months at a time. Eventually, I realised I didn't really need all that other stuff in my checked bag, and I switched to full-time travel with carry-on only in 2012. With my trusty carry-on bag, I've been to the Caribbean, Europe, and North, Central, and South America.

2) What luggage do you use and what do you like or not like about it?

I have a Pacsafe Toursafe 21, and I love it. It's lightweight and has all the anti-theft mechanisms of a Pacsafe bag such as being slash-proof and having solid zippers. I like that it's soft-sided, which not only makes it lighter, but allows you to fit a lot inside, and if you don't have so much to pack, it compresses down. I'm a big fan of wheeled luggage for carry-on, and the Pacsafe has a solid handle and wheels. It feels sturdy and has shown no signs of the abuse I've given it thus far.

3) Do you travel with a day bag in addition to your main carry-on?

Yes. My day bag (a small backpack) houses my computer and other electronics, official documents, and an extra layer of clothing for the plane.

4) What clothes and shoes do you travel with? Are there any particular brands or fabrics that you recommend?

I'm practically the poster child for clothing by Anatomie; they make designer travel clothing for women. It's not cheap, but it packs well, doesn't wrinkle, dries fast, and is very stylish.

5) What technology do you pack?

I have a MacBook Air 11-inch, external hard drive, a Kindle, and a Nokia Lumia 1020 smartphone/camera combo.

6) Do you travel with any luxury items?

I have a small mesa (a Peruvian "power pack" of sorts with crystals and sacred items I've collected), and I also have glow-poi.

7) Did you pack anything that you regretted or got rid of?

When I started travelling full-time, I did so with way more stuff than I needed, and strategically sloughed off stuff along the way. It's a personal learning process for everybody, determining what they really want and need to have.

8) How do you organise your things in your luggage?

One of my favourite packing tools is the Hobo Roll, which organises and compresses an astounding amount of stuff. I'm not sure I could travel with carry-on luggage only without it.

You can follow Nora's travels at The Professional Hobo.

Erin McNeaney

FINAL WORDS

I hope you've found this book useful and are inspired to travel carry-on only for your next trip. It's natural to feel intimidated by the idea, but focus on the benefits—the money, time, and stress you'll save, and the feeling of freedom that will make your travels so much more enjoyable.

Remember that it gets easier over time. If you can't manage to go completely carry-on for your next trip, that's ok. It's a gradual process. Start by reducing what you currently pack, and take a little less each time. At the end of each trip, ask yourself what you could have managed without, and you'll learn what you really need. It's liberating to realise how little you can live with.

Before your next trip, write a packing list and stick to it—don't panic and add extra items at the last minute. Resist those last-minute impulses, and remember that if you truly need it, you can buy it at your destination.

Ultimately, the only way to discover that travelling carry-on only is possible is to challenge yourself to do it. Start with a short trip and see how it goes. What's the worst that can happen?

Mike Sowden says:

"Last week I packed brutally for the first time in my life and squeezed everything for a week's travel into a Belkin laptop backpack. Until I got tough on myself, I'd have never believed it. Carry-on for the win. *waves flag*"

By sharing our packing lists on Never Ending Voyage, we've inspired many people to travel with a carry-on who didn't think it was possible. Everyone raves about the freedom it gives them, and I haven't heard of anyone going back to checking luggage. If we can live out of a carry-on backpack for six years—including our mobile office—can't you manage it for your next week or month-long trip? Try it and you'll never look back.

BONUS PACKING RESOURCES

For more packing resources, visit carryontravels.com, where you can download a packing checklist, see photos of our gear, and find links to the resources and recommended items in this book. I have arranged special discounts exclusively for *The Carry-On Traveller* readers with some of my favourite gear companies, so I recommend checking the resources page before you buy.

For travel tips, gear reviews, and to follow our adventures as digital nomads, you can sign up to receive our monthly newsletter at NeverEndingVoyage.com/newsletter.

If you enjoyed this book, please consider leaving a review on Amazon. Reviews are hugely important to help independent writers like me get found in the store. Even a line or two would make a big difference.

If you have any questions or packing success stories, I'd love to hear them! You can email me at erin@neverendingvoyage.com.

Thank you for reading and happy packing!

Erin

Connect with me:
Website: NeverEndingVoyage.com
Facebook: Facebook.com/NeverEndingVoyage
Twitter: Twitter.com/NevEndingVoyage
Instagram: Instagram.com/NeverEndingVoyage
Pinterest: Pinterest.com/NevEndingVoyage

APPENDIX A: OUR PACKING LIST

Our packing list evolves after regular assessments, and as our clothes are replaced, but the basics stay the same. Here's what we are currently carrying in 2016. You can see our latest list at carryontravels.com.

Luggage

- Tortuga Backpack (Simon)
- Osprey Farpoint 40 (S/M) backpack (Erin)
- Combination locks for backpack zips
- Cotton shoulder bag
- Eagle Creek Pack-It Specter full and half compression cubes (Erin)
- Eagle Creek Pack-It half packing cube (Erin)
- Eagle Creek Pack-It full compression cube (Simon)

Erin's Clothes

- Jeans
- Linen trousers
- Skirt
- 3 dresses
- 3 short-sleeve tops
- Cardigan
- Fleece (The North Face)
- 2 tank tops (1 Athleta Chi tank and 1 H&M for running/yoga)
- Capri leggings (Athleta Be Free Knicker for running/yoga)
- Shorts (Brooks Sherpa 6-inch for running)
- 2 sports bras (1 Victoria's Secret Incredible)
- Runderwear running underwear

- Running socks
- Tankini swimsuit (PrAna Lahari)
- 7 underwear (1 ExOfficio)
- 2 bras
- 2 socks
- Running shoes (Asics Cumulus 17)
- Sports sandals (Merrell Enoki)
- Ballet flats (Brentwood vegan Tieks)
- Sun hat
- Sunglasses and travel case

Simon's Clothes

- Jeans (Levis 511)
- Trousers (Bluffs)
- Shorts (Craghoppers Kiwi)
- 3 t-shirts
- Short-sleeve shirt
- Long-sleeve shirt
- Fleece
- Swimming shorts
- 7 underwear (1 ExOfficio)
- 4 socks
- Hiking shoes (Scarpa Margarita GTX)
- Sandals (Teva Terra Fi Lite)
- Sunglasses and travel case

Toiletries

- Toiletry bag (Lifeventure Ultralite Wash Holdall)
- Small zip-lock bag for liquids when flying (usually we fit our liquids into one bag between us)
- Suncream (100 ml Riemann P20)
- Lush shampoo bar + tin
- Toothbrush each + head cover
- Toothpaste (usually a 50 ml tube)
- Solid deodorant (Salt of the Earth 50 g)
- Lip balm (small solid tube)
- Hand sanitiser (50 ml bottle)

- Shaving oil (Simon, 15 ml bottle)
- Razor each + 2 or 3 spare blades
- Hairbrush (travel-size)
- Nail clippers
- Tweezers
- Mooncup (Erin)
- Hairbands and clips (Erin)

Sometimes I'll add these extra items in 50-100 ml (2-3 oz) bottles when needed:

- Moisturiser
- Hair conditioner
- Insect repellant

Medical

- Ibuprofen
- Loperamide (Imodium) - For traveller's diarrhoea.
- Dimenhydrinate (Dramamine) - For motion sickness.
- Plasters (Band-Aids)
- Prescription medications
- Ciprofloxacin antibiotic - We sometimes have this on hand for severe cases of traveller's diarrhoea.
- Antihistamine - Simon has allergies, so we sometimes carry these.

Electronics

Laptops and Accessories

- MacBook Pro Retina 15-inch laptop + Incase neoprene case + charger (Simon)
- MacBook Air 11-inch laptop + Incase neoprene case + charger (Erin)
- Western Digital My Passport 1 TB hard drive (Simon)
- Seagate Backup Plus Slim 1 TB hard drive (Erin)
- Small mouse (Simon)
- International travel power adapter
- USB flash drive
- HDMI cable

- Eagle Creek e-Tools Organizer Pro for storing cables and accessories

Photography (Erin)

- Olympus OM-D EM-5 mirrorless camera + Tamrac 3440 Rally Micro shoulder bag
- Olympus 14-42 mm kit lens
- Panasonic 20 mm f1.7 pancake lens
- Charger + 3 batteries
- Sandisk Extreme 16GB SD cards x 2
- USB cable for uploading photos
- Lens pen for cleaning

iPhones, iPad, Kindle, Watch

- iPhone 6 128 GB unlocked + Apple EarPods (Simon)
- iPhone 5 64 GB unlocked + Apple EarPods + Shocksock neoprene sleeve (Erin)
- iPad Pro Wi-Fi 32 GB + neoprene case (Simon)
- Kindle Paperwhite 3G + USB cable + neoprene sleeve (Erin)
- Apple Watch Sport 42mm + USB cable (Simon)
- Apple Pencil for drawing on the iPad Pro
- Plate stand for the iPad
- Apple lightning cables x 2 + USB power adapter
- Headphone splitter

Miscellaneous

- Travel towel (Simon)
- Sarong (Erin)
- AeroPress coffee maker (Simon's current experiment. He got rid of the funnel, stirrer, and filter holder to save space.)
- Petzl Tikka 2 head torch (headlamp)
- Small roll of duct tape
- BioEars earplugs (Erin)
- Eye mask (Erin)
- Lifeventure mini retractable cable lock
- Tiny sewing kit
- Pens

- Small dry bag
- Few zip-lock bags
- Toilet paper (a little folded up)
- Moo business cards

Documents and Money

- Passport
- Dollars
- 2 debit and 3 credit cards each
- Card reader for online banking (issued by our bank for secure access)
- Driving licence
- International driving licence (when needed)
- Photocopies of passport
- Passport photos (for visa applications)
- Vaccination card
- Yellow fever vaccination card
- Scuba diving certification card
- European Health Insurance Card (when in Europe)
- Money belt
- Wallet (Simon) including a copy of our passports and travel insurance details

APPENDIX B: OTHER PACKING LISTS

Packing and Gear Websites

For carry-on packing tips, gear reviews, and sample packing lists, see these websites (links can be found on carryontravels.com):

Packsmith - The creators of the Tortuga Backpack have a useful blog with tips on packing light and sample packing lists for many types of trips.

Travel Fashion Girl - Do you want to look stylish and travel light? This is the site for you, with advice on everything from makeup to the best travel shoes and packing lists for every climate and destination.

Her Packing List - Packing advice for women with gear reviews and example packing lists (although not all are carry-on only).

Stylish Travel Girl - Another resource for packing light with style.

One Bag - A detailed guide to travelling light.

Snarky Nomad - Comprehensive reviews of (mostly male) travel gear such as the best backpacks, travel trousers, down jackets, and more, as well as packing lists for ultra light travel.

The Wirecutter - This isn't a travel website, but the technology and gear reviews are helpful when choosing what to buy for a trip. Unlike other tech review sites, they go through all the options for a certain item (laptop, camera, smartphone, etc.) and choose the best one—they do the work for you, which makes the decision much easier. See their travel section for relevant recommendations.

Other Carry-On Packing Lists

For inspiration to travel light, see these packing lists by other carry-on travellers. You'll notice that everyone has their own style and packs what's important to them (although I see some common items like the MacBook Air, Kindle, merino wool clothes, and Eagle Creek packing cubes). Don't follow anyone else's packing list to the letter (including ours)—use it as a guide and adapt to your personal preferences.

Couple Packing Lists

Till the Money Runs Out - Tom and Jenny have been living out of a backpack for years. Here they share their packing list for four months in Mexico. They have the same Tortuga/Osprey Farpoint 40 backpack combination as we do, and fit a surprising amount in their bags including plenty of clothes, tech gear, and even a full-size feather pillow!

Camera & Carry On - Shannon and Michael travelled for six months to all climates with a carry-on roller suitcase plus a small backpack.

Live Your Legend - Scott and Chelsea packed for a year around the world in 45-litre backpacks. They prioritised technical clothing that looks normal and electronics for working on the road. Chelsea managed to fit in plenty of clothes, toiletries, and makeup.

Almost Landing - Mandy and Chris travelled for nine weeks in Europe with a carry-on roller suitcase.

Bolivian Life - What to pack for Bolivia (applies to any South America trip) where the climate varies and the focus is on outdoor activities. Brigid even packs a yoga mat.

Ever in Transit - Cassie and Kevin travel with 40-litre backpacks and share their women's and men's packing lists for a trip to South America.

Drea Castillo - Drea and Eliot travelled for six months, including trekking in Nepal, with a 40-litre backpack each. They preferred technical clothing and managed with just hiking boots and flip-flops.

Viajar y Amar - Anne and Mike are a nomadic couple who travel with a small backpack and messenger bag each.

Anywhereism - Mirje and Antti are another digital nomad couple who work on the road.

Indefinite Adventure - Sam and Zab are a gay couple who travelled for two years in South America and Europe.

Nomad is Beautiful - Despite their small backpacks, Ivana and Gianni travel with lots of photography gear.

Female Packing Lists

The Yoga Nomads - Anne is a nomadic yoga teacher who manages to fit a good amount of stuff in her Osprey Farpoint 40 backpack, including a yoga mat and towel, makeup, contact lens solution, and electronics.

One World One Year - Britnee travelled for a year to multiple climates with a 43-litre backpack. She used an iPad mini and keyboard instead of a laptop, managed to fit in a travel-size hair dryer and straighteners (although she's not sure they were worth it), and regretted not packing jeans.

Take Your Big Trip - Kristin packed for cold and hot weather on her trip to Bhutan with options for hiking and dressing up in cities. She travels with an Osprey Contrail roller suitcase and a small daypack.

Making It Anywhere - Mish is a digital nomad who travels with her partner Rob. She shares her detailed packing list with the brands of clothes she wears.

Burger Abroad - Amanda is a full-time traveller and housesitter who travels impressively light with only 5 kg (11 lb) in her 12-litre backpack. She loves the ultralight MacBook and uses her iPhone 6 as a camera.

Life in Limbo - Steph backpacked through Europe for three months in multiple climates. She had plenty of clothes and managed her photos with her iPad Mini.

Dream Travel Girl - Laia travelled around the world on a low budget with a 35-litre backpack and small shoulder bag.

Meet Daria - A year-long trip with a Tortuga Backpack, which shows the Tortuga can work for taller women as well as men.

Ali Adventures - Ali has travelled many times with a carry-on. This is her packing list for a seven-week trip to Europe that included colder weather. She travels with a 40-litre backpack, purse, and packable daypack.

Off the Blue Print - Allison travels ultra light with a 19-litre Tom Bihn Synapse backpack.

Male Packing Lists

Snarky Nomad - Packing list for a month in Guatemala with a 25-litre Tom Bihn backpack.

Breakaway Backpacker - Jaime travelled for two years with a carry-on backpack, and this is his updated packing list for his second round-the-world trip.

Paul Austin - Long-term travel in Southeast Asia with just a 19-litre Tom Bihn backpack, despite fitting in plenty of electronics and even an AeroPress coffee maker. Paul is a fan of merino wool clothing and manages with two pairs of underwear!

James Turner - This nomadic designer travels with a 26-litre backpack even though he needs a 15-inch MacBook Pro and other tech gear for his business.

Tropical MBA - Dan is another digital nomad who has been travelling in SE Asia with a Minaal backpack plus laptop bag since 2008.

Fred Perrotta - The founder of Tortuga shares his packing list for guys wanting to dress smart in Europe—with only nine items of clothing.

Tim Richards - A Lonely Planet travel writer shares the ultra light packing list he has used on multiple trips to Europe. His top tip is the Rule of Three, where he packs no more than three of any item of clothing. He writes with his iPad and keyboard and uses his iPhone as a camera.

Andrew Hyde - An ultra light packing list from a guy who travelled for 25 days to three countries with a laptop bag. He later sold everything he owned and lived out of a backpack with just 15 items.

No Baggage Challenge - Rolf Potts travelled around the world for six weeks with no luggage at all! He packed essential items in the pockets of his jacket and cargo trousers.

Cold Weather Packing Lists

Many of the packing lists above include clothing for multiple climates, but these lists are specifically for winter travel:

Be My Travel Muse - Kristin travels with a carry-on for a winter trip to Europe and still looks stylish.

Travel Fashion Girl - Another fashionable female packing list for cold weather.

Oh Happy Day - How to look great in Paris in the winter.

Her Packing List - A packing list for 28 days in Lapland with temperatures as low as -38ºC (-36ºF)! Although this list isn't strictly carry-on only (she had a 55-litre Osprey Farpoint), it would be easy to adapt it, especially by wearing the bulkiest clothes and using compression bags.

Snarky Nomad - A simple layering system for cold weather travel.

Family Packing Lists

Where's Sharon - Sharon, her husband, and their two children aged three and five, travelled for over three months in Europe and three weeks in Sri Lanka. The adults have backpacks and the kids pull (or ride on) fun Trunki suitcases.

Her Packing List - Renata shares her packing list for a month-long trip around the UK with her three daughters aged seven, nine, and twelve years old. Each member of the family had a carry-on backpack with wheels.

Packsmith - Jenn travelled for five days in Central America with her husband and four kids with one Tortuga Backpack for all six of them.

Camping Packing Lists

Adventure Alan - This site focuses on hiking trips rather than travel, but if you are planning to camp on your travels, you'll find recommendations for ultralight camping gear. His packing lists for a variety of trips are very detailed.

APPENDIX C: AIRLINE CARRY-ON LUGGAGE RESTRICTIONS

These are the size and weight limits for your main piece of cabin baggage on major airlines as of 2016. A smaller personal item is also allowed unless I've stated otherwise—check with the airline for the size.

Luggage rules do change, so check the airline's website before you fly.

North America

US airlines have the most generous carry-on allowances, often with no weight limit.

Aeromexico: 22 x 14 x 9 inches (56 x 36 x 23 cm), 22 lb (10 kg).

Air Canada: 22 x 16 x 9 inches (55 x 40 x 23 cm), 22 lb (10 kg).

Alaska Airlines: 24 x 17 x 10 inches (61 x 43 x 25 cm), no weight limit.

American Airlines: 22 x 14 x 9 inches (56 x 36 x 23 cm), no weight limit.

Delta: 22 x 14 x 9 inches (56 x 36 x 23 cm), no weight limit.

JetBlue Airways: 24 x 16 x 10 inches (61 x 41 x 25 cm), no weight limit.

Southwest Airlines: 24 x 16 x 10 inches (61 x 41 x 25 cm), no weight limit.

* Spirit Airlines: 16 x 14 x 12 inches (40 x 35 x 30 cm). You can also pay to take a larger carry-on of 22 x 18 x 10 inches (56 x 46 x 25 cm). No weight limit.

United: 22 x 14 x 9 inches (56 x 36 x 23 cm), no weight limit.

Virgin America: 24 x 16 x 10 inches (61 x 41 x 25 cm), 30 lb (14 kg).

* **Volaris:** Two personal items of 16 x 16 x 10 inches (40 x 40 x 25 cm) are allowed, and you can pay for a larger carry-on of 22 x 16 x 13 inches (57 x 40 x 33 cm) with a weight of 22 lb (10 kg).

Europe

European airlines tend to be stricter than US airlines, especially about luggage weight and personal items (which are often not allowed). Avoid getting your bag weighed if possible (see my tips in 3 - Understanding Airline Restrictions).

Aeroflot: 56 x 36 x 23 cm (22 x 14 x 9 inches), 10 kg (22 lb).

Air Berlin: 55 x 40 x 20 cm (22 x 16 x 8 inches), 8 kg (18 lb). Personal item can be a laptop or handbag up to 2 kg (4.4 lb).

Air France: 55 x 35 x 25 cm (22 x 14 x 10 inches), 12 kg (26 lb).

Alitalia: 55 x 35 x 25 cm (22 x 14 x 10 inches), 8 kg (18 lb).

British Airways: 56 x 45 x 25 cm (22 x 18 x 10 inches), 23 kg (51 lb).

EasyJet: 56 x 45 x 25 cm (22 x 18 x 10 inches), no weight limit. No personal item unless you're an easyJet Plus cardholder, Flexi fare, Upfront, or Extra Legroom customer.

Flybe: 55 x 35 x 20 cm (22 x 14 x 8 inches), 10 kg (22 lb). No personal item unless you pay for the more expensive All In ticket.

Jet2: 56 x 45 x 25 cm (22 x 18 x 10 inches), 10 kg (22 lb). No personal item.

KLM: 55 x 35 x 25 cm (22 x 14 x 10 inches), 12 kg (26 lb).

Lufthansa: 55 x 40 x 23 cm (22 x 16 x 9 inches), 8 kg (18 lb).

Norwegian: 55 x 40 x 23 cm (22 x 16 x 9 inches), 10 kg (22 lb).

Ryanair: 55 x 40 x 20 cm (22 x 16 x 8 inches), 10 kg (22 lb). Only 90 cabin bags per flight, so line up early to board or purchase Priority Boarding.

Scandinavian Airlines: 55 x 40 x 23 cm (22 x 16 x 9 inches), 8 kg (18 lb).

Turkish Airlines: 55 x 40 x 23 cm (22 x 16 x 9 inches), 8 kg (18 lb).

Virgin Atlantic: 56 x 36 x 23 cm (22 x 14 x 9 inches), 10 kg (22 lb).

Asia

The weight restrictions on airlines in Asia are even stricter than in Europe.

Air Asia: 56 x 36 x 23 cm (22 x 14 x 9 inches), 7 kg (15 lb).

Air China: 55 x 40 x 20 cm (22 x 16 x 8 inches), 5 kg (11 lb). No personal item.

Air India: 55 x 40 x 20 cm (22 x 16 x 8 inches), 8 kg (18 lb).

Cathay Pacific: 56 x 36 x 23 cm (22 x 14 x 9 inches), 7 kg (15 lb).

Emirates: 55 x 38 x 20 cm (22 x 15 x 8 inches), 7 kg (15 lb). No personal item.

Japan Airlines: 55 x 40 x 25 cm (22 x 16 x 10 inches), 10 kg (22 lb).

Jet Airways: 55 x 35 x 25 cm (22 x 14 x 10 inches), 7 kg (15 lb).

* **Lion Air:** 40 x 30 x 20 cm (16 x 12 x 8 inches), 7 kg (15 lb). No personal item except a small purse or camera.

Qatar Airways: 50 x 37 x 25 cm (20 x 15 x 10 inches), 7 kg (15 lb). No personal item except a small purse, briefcase, or camera.

Singapore Airlines: 56 x 36 x 23 cm (22 x 14 x 9 inches), 7 kg (15 lb).

Thai Airways: 56 x 45 x 25 cm (22 x 18 x 10 inches), 7 kg (15 lb).

Tigerair (Asia): 54 x 38 x 23 cm (21 x 15 x 9 inches), 10 kg (22 lb) including personal item.

Oceania

As in Asia, weight limits are low.

Air New Zealand: Not exceeding total linear dimensions (length + width + height) of 118 cm (46.5 inches), 7 kg (15 lb).

* **Jetstar:** 56 x 36 x 23 cm (22 x 14 x 9 inches), 7 kg (15 lb). No personal item except a small purse or coat (included in weight allowance). They regularly weigh hand luggage at the gate and charge high fees to check in overweight bags.

Qantas: 56 x 36 x 23 cm (22 x 14 x 9 inches), 7 kg (15 lb).

* **Tigerair (Australia):** 54 x 38 x 23 cm (21 x 15 x 9 inches), 7 kg (15 lb). No personal item except a small purse, tablet, or coat (included in weight allowance). You can pay for Cabin+ to increase the weight limit to 12 kg.

* **Virgin Australia (Domestic and short haul):** Two small bags 48 x 34 x 23 cm (19 x 13 x 9 inches), combined weight 7 kg (15 lb).

Virgin Australia (International long haul): 56 x 36 x 23 cm (22 x 14 x 9 inches), 7 kg (15 lb).

* These airlines have the strictest carry-on luggage requirements—be especially careful that your luggage meets them.

ACKNOWLEDGMENTS

Writing a book is very different from writing blog posts (however lengthy mine tend to be), and my first book venture wouldn't have been possible without the help and support of a number of people.

Thank you to my beta readers, who provided essential early feedback, helped me improve the book, and kept me going with their kind words: Miriam Abraham, Tatyana Astanovsky, Elizabeth Bagwell, Jason Ball, Asha Bhatia, Katherine Buechler, Sophie Dourambeis, John Farnsworth, Colette File, Mike Gallagher, Etty Green, Carol Guttery, Dani Heinrich, Kathy Johnson, Tricia Krohn, Jenny Krones, Laurie Linden, Tomas Machart, Christine Milton, Anne Marie Parker, David Parker, Jack Peacock, Peter Pecksen, Carla Piedrahita, Ruth Rehak, Caitlin Rielly, Bec Robbie, Kate Savory, Ken Schellin, Denise Sigworth, Betsy Talbot, Cristina Thomas, Dieter Wittman, and Ellen Wittmann.

My proofreader, Mary Lynam, did a fantastic job finding inconsistencies and errors.

A big thank you to Warren and Betsy Talbot, who inspired me with their many wonderful self-published books and patiently answered all my questions.

Most of all, thank you to Simon, my partner in life, work, and carry-on travel. He formatted the book, created the online resources page, and kept me sane during this often challenging process. He makes everything possible.

Made in the USA
Coppell, TX
27 November 2019